PRAISE FOR

NO PRETTY PICTURES

"Neither sentimental nor exploitative. . . . The integrity of the storytelling is in the narrowness of the child's viewpoint, the physical immediacy, the bewilderment. The truth is that nothing makes sense."
—*The New York Times*

"Lobel brings to these dramatic experiences an artist's sensibility for the telling detail, a seemingly unvarnished memory and heartstopping candor."
—*Publishers Weekly* (starred review)

"Lobel's ebullient, gorgeously colored illustrated books give no hint of her dark, terrifying childhood. . . . There's a visceral physicalness to her memories of the terror and in the elementals she celebrated when she was safe." —ALA *Booklist* (starred review)

"Lobel is an exceptional writer. Almost miraculously she retains little Aneta's perspective as she puts down exactly what she saw and felt at the time. She does not embellish, she does not invent. . . . It is a fascinating book told with unadorned authority and conviction. *No Pretty Pictures* is pretty remarkable."

—*The Washington Post*

"Anita Lobel's memoir of her traumatic years in Poland spent under the threat of annihilation by the Nazis is notable both as an account of survival and as a revelation of a remarkable human being. . . . True, there are no pretty pictures, but there are moments of description that are intensely visual and vivid, and will not be easily forgotten." —*The Horn Book*

"What distinguishes this Holocaust memoir . . . is the author's scrupulous honesty to her perceptions as a child. . . . Lobel projects herself not as a hero nor even a victim, but a determined, sometimes irascible survivor."

—*Bulletin of the Center for Children's Books*

"Lobel has written a haunting, honest, and ultimately life-affirming account of her childhood years in Nazi-occupied Poland. . . . The author's words are simple and straightforward, even when she describes the horror of life in the camp or the fear and loneliness of being separated from her family and nanny."

—*School Library Journal*

"This is an inexpressibly sad book about a young girl who missed her childhood, yet survived to say that her life 'has been good. I want more.'"
—*Kirkus Reviews*

"Told in clear, strong prose that lets the reader imagine what this experience was like for a sharply observant, spirited child." —*Riverbank Review*

HONORS AND AWARDS FOR
NO PRETTY PICTURES

National Book Award Finalist

New York Times Notable Book

ALA Best Book for Young Adults

Publishers Weekly Best Book

ALA *Booklist* Top of the List Editors' Choice

Bulletin of the Center for Children's Books
Blue Ribbon Book

New York Public Library Book for the Teen Age

Riverbank Review Children's Book of Distinction

VOYA Nonfiction Honor List

Children's Literature Choice List

CCBC Choice Book

IRA Notable Book for a Global Society

Judy Lopez Memorial Award

Orbis Pictus Honor Book

Sydney Taylor Honor Book

Golden Kite Honor Book

NO PRETTY PICTURES

A CHILD OF WAR

Sweden, 1945

ANITA LOBEL

A Greenwillow Book

☾ Collins

An Imprint of HarperCollins*Publishers*

Collins is an imprint of HarperCollins Publishers.

All photographs and illustrative material appear courtesy of
Anita Lobel.
The "matzos in the doll carriage" episode in Chapter 3 also
appears in *Tikvah: Perspectives on Human Rights; A
Compilation of Images and Observations by Illustrators of
Books for Children* (1998: Thomas J. Dodd Research Center,
University of Connecticut, Storrs, CT).

Library of Congress Cataloging-in-Publication Data
Lobel, Anita, (date).
No pretty pictures : a child of war / Anita Lobel.
p. cm.
"Greenwillow Books."
Summary: The author, known as an illustrator of children's
books, describes her experiences as a Polish Jew during World
War II and for years in Sweden afterwards.
ISBN: 978-0-06-156589-2 (pbk.)
[1. Lobel, Anita—Childhood and youth—Juvenile literature.
2. Jews—Poland—Kraków—Biography—Juvenile literature.
3. Holocaust, Jewish (1939-1945)—Poland—Kraków—Personal
narratives—Juvenile literature. 4. Jewish children in the Holocaust—
Juvenile literature. 5. Holocaust survivors. 6. Kraków
(Poland)—Ethnic relations—Juvenile literature.] I. Title.
DS135.P63 L63 1998 940.53/18'092—dc21 [B] 97048392

09 10 11 12 13 CG/RRDH 10 9 8 7 6 5 4 3 2

Typography by Victoria Jamieson
First Collins edition, 2008

FOR MY BROTHER
AND TO THE MEMORY OF NIANIA

———◦◦◦◦———

A NOTE ON THE NAMES IN THIS BOOK:

The form of Polish nouns changes when they are used diminutively. For example, the more endearing form of Mama is Mamusia, of Niania (the author's nanny) is Nianiusia, and the diminutive of Father is Tatuś. When used in direct address, the noun takes the ending -u, for example, Mamusiu, Nianiusiu, Tatusiu.

The author's given name in Polish was Aneta. Other forms include the formal Anna, or Hana, or Hanka. Throughout this book you will see her name as Hanusia and Hanusiu (when addressed directly). Later in Sweden, the name evolved into Anita.

———◦◦◦◦———

CONTENTS

———∞∞∞———

Kraków, 1936

PROLOGUE

I WAS BORN IN KRAKÓW, POLAND. IN A WRONG place at a wrong time. I have lived in America, in New York City, since I came here as a teenager. I was an art student then. I have been a painter, a fabric designer. I am a picture maker.

For over thirty years the making and thinking up of pictures for children's books have occupied my professional life. I did not spring full blown into this calling. But the opportunity presented itself way back in the year 1964, when Susan Hirschman, an inspired editor and publisher and a dear, dear friend, suggested that I try a picture book. She must have known something I was not smart enough to think of myself. It has been a gentle as well as an exacting craft for a visual artist to pursue.

I have a vague memory of being read to by my nanny or some other grown-up when I was very little. By the time I was five years old I knew how to read. I have a vivid recollection of the moment when, on the oblong, thin, flimsy, brownish paper that resembled newsprint more than a page of an illustrated book, I deciphered one complete sentence in Polish. *"Ola i Olek maja jajko."* ("Ola and Olek have an egg.") There was a picture of a girl and a boy happily contemplating an egg poised in an eggcup in front of them on a table.

I remember being told that I was a spoiled little girl. If Hitler's armies had not heaped destruction on the promises and futures of our not wealthy but comfortable lives, there was no reason to doubt that I was on my way to the conventionally polished existence of a Jewish middle-class girl in a city of Eastern Europe. As a very little girl I remember my parents, especially my mother, circling the periphery of my life. I adored my father, an elegant, well-dressed gentleman with a wonderful, clean smell of perfume on his hair and neck. He doted on me. The person who was by my side on a moment-to-moment basis was my nanny. I loved her dearly. Swept into the events of World War II, which no grown-up around me could control, I soon began to take for granted that life was always lived on the edge or in the shadow of terrible threats.

To this day I am suspicious when reasonable everyday life proceeds at a sleepy pace. Then I find myself
stirring up an artificial crisis, a tempest in a teapot.

I was barely five years old when the war began.
Only when I was much older did the horrors and terrible losses of fully conscious people during all those
years of terror dawn on me. As a person who has lived
a life with rights to make reasonable and foolish deci-
sions, who has been fed and clothed and has collected
possessions and memories, who has had quiet times
and the reassurance of schedules and daily routines
and vacations and work and Christmas, I mourn for
all those who were grown, thinking people and who
were truly capable of knowing and feeling that which
was torn from them.

Childhoods are difficult even in the best of times.
I look at children in happy times, and I see little
people with wisdom in their eyes at the mercy of big
people who don't know what they are doing. I suppose it is too fanciful to compare a life lived placidly
with parents in a pleasant house with a living room
and bedrooms and bathrooms and toys and a kitchen
with a refrigerator packed with food, with a life
trudging and surviving on the landscape of war. But
it is also wearisome as well as dangerous to cloak and
sanctify oneself with the pride of victimhood. I have
spent many, many more years living well, occupied

with doing happy and interesting things, than I spent ducking the Nazis or being a refugee.

Over the years many people have asked me to write the recollections of the early years of my life. I have balked. I have resisted. In writing down this story, I have reached to a time when everything in the world I lived in was being trampled on and destroyed. A time from which I have very few pretty pictures to remember.

POLAND

My mother and father smile at me in the baby carriage. I must be about four or five months old. Kraków, 1934.

FROM OUR BALCONY ON A SEPTEMBER DAY A long time ago, I watched the Germans march into the city where we lived. They stepped in unison, in shiny boots, with sunlight glinting on helmets and bouncing off bayonets. They sang a marching song. I did not understand the words that echoed between the buildings. Pushing my head through the bars of our crowded balcony to see the soldiers better, I held on tightly to my *niania's* (nanny's) hand. *"Niemcy, Niemcy"* ("Germans, Germans"), she muttered and sighed. My mother and father were there, and many other people. "No! No! They are French!" I heard people say. "Surely they must be French." It was a warm and beautiful day. There was music and promise in the air.

The back of the large apartment building where we lived faced a square courtyard. Here balconies were long walkways that extended the whole length of the building. We sometimes saw our neighbor, a Hasid, in his long black coat and round saucerlike hat edged in fur, rushing by our back windows on his way to the elevator. He turned corners, his beard flying in the wind. "Jews!" I would hear Niania mutter.

My father was the owner of a chocolate factory. He was not a Hasid. But every morning he wrapped his head in thin black leather straps that ended in a small square box that rested on his forehead. The ends of the straps were tied around his wrists. He put a white shawl with black stripes around his shoulders and faced a window that led to the back balcony. He mumbled and rocked back and forth. Under the leather straps on his head he wore a tight hairnet clasped on the side with a buckle. After he finished his mumblings, he unwrapped the straps, kissed them, and wound them back into the box he had taken off his head. He went to another room and came out elegantly dressed in a fine gray suit with a white shirt, a tie, and a boutonniere in his lapel. His hair was beautifully slicked down. He wore shiny black shoes and often spats. He smelled nice when he kissed me good-bye.

Then, one morning, he was gone and did not come back. He had kissed me in the night, and I did not

4

know it. I looked for his shoes. I could not find his smell, and I cried.

One afternoon that October I was standing by the window that looked out on the courtyard. Something happened. I don't know how it happened. I did not see the beginning of it. Niania cried: "Don't look! Don't look!" She tried to pull me away from the window. "Come away from there!" Six floors below an open window facing our part of the building, several people were surrounding something on the ground. I could see a dark liquid slowly appear on the cement courtyard. Without really knowing, I knew what all this was.

Whenever I ran and fell, banging my head, a black smell curled around in my head. No, even before, before the pain really began. Before I had had time to burst into my childish wail, an oily pungency flushed the inside of my head and spread through my mouth and my nostrils.

Once, before the German soldiers had even come, I had been walking with Niania in the middle of the city, near a place called the Rondel. Into this remaining part of a medieval tower surrounded by a waterless moat, two motorcyclists had crashed. The railing had been bent and broken in several places. I saw no bodies. But before Niania hurried me away, I had seen the dark, dark red pools of liquid in the moat. There had been the noise that sirens and policemen and *droszki* (horse-drawn carriages) and horses made. And in my head there had been the smell of it all.

The shape on the ground of our courtyard had been covered. The edges of the blanket fanned out neatly. The puddle of blackish red liquid that slowly seeped out from under the blanketed mound was growing larger. A high-heeled shoe had fallen off one foot that could just barely be seen under the covering. And that smell was in my head again.

A blue late-afternoon sky cradled the roofs of my Eastern European city when Niania closed the drapes.

A little later I sneaked back to the window. It was dark now. I could no longer see a stain. There was no blanket on the ground. The shoe was gone. The courtyard was empty. There was nothing.

2

THE NIGHT THE NAZIS CAME TO OUR APARTMENT in the winter of 1939, their guns were politely pointed at the ceiling. There were three of them. Niania took my brother and me into our large kitchen. She held us both by the hand and stayed with us. I heard booted steps thumping from room to room. I heard Mother speak to the soldiers in German. She didn't sound scared. Maybe in German people don't sound scared. I couldn't understand what anyone was saying. There was no shouting. I waited for the soldiers to come into the kitchen, but they never did. We stayed there quietly with Niania and our two servant girls. They stood stiffly by the stove, never looking at us. Nobody spoke. When we heard the front door close, we went back to Mother.

The heavy wardrobe where we hung our coats was wide open. "They took my furs," Mother said. "And all the silver." The open cupboards of the dining room armoire were bare. The holiday candlesticks and the fancy silver coffeepot and teapot were gone.

Not long before, I had been allowed to sit at my first Passover Seder with the grown-ups. I was almost five years old. It seemed like an important thing. I sat next to my father at the long mahogany table with a white tablecloth on it. And all the different plates and glasses. I liked the taste of the bitter herbs. And the egg dipped in salt water. My father hadn't put on the leather straps and the striped shawl the way he did when he rocked and mumbled in the mornings. At the Seder table he wore a small round silk cap on his head and half sang words that I did not understand from a book.

I had a new blue velvet dress with a white lace collar. I had been allowed to stay up late. When all the invited uncles and aunts and Grandmother and Grandfather were leaving, I was alone in the dining room. I climbed up and down on chairs and drank what was left of the wine in the red goblets. The sweet drink tasted good and made me feel as if I were riding a carousel. Then Mother saw what I was doing and roughly took me away.

Now the floor in the narrow hallway that led to

the dining room was bare. The long beautiful rug, with its center of curved dark red designs shaped like snails and the garland of many colored flowers between the stripes of the border, was gone.

"Yes, they took the kilim, too," Mother said. "Just rolled it up and took it away."

My little three-year-old brother thought *kilim* was a funny word. Whenever I wanted to hear him laugh, I'd say, "Let's play on the kilim." We would roll back and forth on the long rug. My brother couldn't stop laughing. Often the kilim giggles gave way to coughing and choking. Niania had to put us to bed. She made us lie there quietly until our silly gasps stopped erupting and we had calmed down. Now, where our funny rug had always been, there was a shadow on the naked floor. And some dust. When we walked on the bare parquet, our steps made hollow sounds. It felt as if there were a hole in the floor.

"They demanded jewelry," Mother said. "I told them I didn't have any. Why would they have believed me?"

The Nazis had worked neatly and fast. The apartment just looked emptier. Not as if robbers had been in it. "I'm sure they'll be back," Mother sighed.

"Where is Tatuś?" I asked. "Why did Papa leave us?"

"He had to. Jewish men are in more danger from the Nazis than women and children."

"Is he safe now, Mamusiu?" I started to cry. I missed my father terribly. I missed our special Sunday walks, when both of us wore hats and gloves and went to the pastry shop together. I missed his telephone calls. "*Servus* [Hello], Hanusiu," he always said. I held the white-and-gold receiver, letting my father's voice flow into my ear.

"Yes, yes, he is safe." Mother sounded tired and irritated. How could she know he was safe? Had she heard from Father and kept it a secret?

Mother had false papers that proved she wasn't Jewish. She didn't wear the yellow star and was permitted to work. She had bought the fake identity papers from someone who knew how to make them. The document looked very real with seals and stamps and Mother's photograph with a stranger's name under it. Every day Mother came home to tell us that someone she had worked with was no longer in the office. Every day we waited for a letter from my father. Nothing came.

There were new rumors every day. Warnings of danger. Like the red tin signal arms on the railway embankment at the end of our street, which I had so liked looking up at when I stood with Niania waiting for the train to come into view and quickly whiz by on its way to the central station.

One morning in the tiny room off the kitchen the

cots stood empty. The two Polish servant girls who had worked for us had left during the night without explanation or good-bye. They had taken some of the cooking pots and many other things from the kitchen with them.

"Why?" Mother sighed. "Didn't we always treat them well?"

"*Pani* [Madame] has to understand that it is not safe anymore for us to stay with Jews," Niania said.

I knew that Niania blamed all Jews for the torture and death of Christ. She didn't like the Hasidic Jew with the fur hat we used to see rushing by the back balconies. She sneered at the kosher dishes in the family household. In the kitchen she kept a special little pan that she used for cooking bits of bacon. I loved the smell of the cracklings she prepared for herself. And she always shared them with me and my brother.

Mother and Father had argued with Niania about Christian things. There was a time when Niania left. A new nanny came. The first night she was with us she gave me a bath. I hated the way she touched me and poured water over my head and down my back. She was not my *niania*. I screamed and cried so much that I frightened Mother and Father. I got my *niania* back.

My parents had to let Niania have her way. Over

my bed she had hung a picture of an angel guard-
ing two children crossing a bridge over a treacherous
ravine. On December 6, St. Nicholas Day, my brother
and I found the large decorated gingerbread cookies
baked in the image of the saint under our pillows.
Niania showed us how to make garlands out of colorful pieces of paper. She bought beautiful paper angels
and bright shiny balls. She convinced Father to let
her have some of the special chocolates that had gold
strings for hanging. In the nursery my brother and I
woke up to a magical sight waiting for us on Christmas morning.

And now when everyone was fleeing, Niania was
not afraid of staying right there with us. Perhaps she
had selected us to be her special kind of Jews.

One afternoon Mother came home crying. She stood
in the middle of the empty spot where the kilim
rug had been and cried the way I had never seen a
grown-up cry. "They have taken them. They were
put on a transport. Mother and Father have been
deported. And my sister . . ."

Her sister. That was the aunt who sometimes came
to stay with me in the evenings. She read me stories.
Now in the whispering of the grown-ups I began
to hear over and over again the words *transported,
deported, concentration camp.* And *liquidation.*

Somewhere there must be a terrible place. A barren area with no light. With leafless trees and no blue in the sky. Where these words stopped being just words and became real things.

Not too long before my grandparents and my aunt were deported I had sat on a park bench between Niania and my grandmother. The trees were losing their leaves, and Niania was complaining of a headache from the traffic smells. Grandmother was telling me something. I didn't pay any attention to what she was saying. I was busy looking at the cold sore, right in the center of her upper lip, A crack, pink with thin, dry bluish lines at the edges, opened and closed as she talked. In two places across her chest her sweater was unbuttoned. And I saw that one button was missing.

When deportation ended, would Grandmother come back? When I saw her again, would the crack on her lip be healed? And what of my mother's sister? My aunt. When was she coming back from the deportation to read to me again? The tall, stern man I called Grandfather, my mother's *tatuś* (papa), had never been very friendly. He never said much to me or played with me. On a table by her bed Mother kept a photograph of him. He was a young man in the picture. On his head a four-cornered cap with a brim was set at a careful angle. One hand was stiffly placed in the jacket pocket of his Polish soldier's uniform.

Maybe he was deported so that he could be a soldier again. He would fight and make the Nazis go away. I didn't understand. I was afraid to ask what it really meant that all these people had been taken away to be "deported." I was only surprised that my mother could cry that way. The way I had cried one morning when my father was not there.

3

MOTHER AND NIANIA DECIDED THAT MY BROTHER
and I were no longer safe in the city. They heard that
in the countryside there might not be so much danger
from the Nazis. With her false papers Mother would
get by in Kraków. We should try to stay away until
the danger stopped. Until Father came back. Until the
war was over. Probably it would not be for such a long
time.

We left with Niania on a bus for the village of
Łapanów, a place where we used to go for short stays
in the summer before the war began. My father's
relatives lived there. They had a house on the village
square, and they were the owners of a beer hall.

There was Babcia, the other grandmother. Babcia
never left her chair on wheels. She had funny-looking

hair, parted in the middle. It always sat on her head the same way. She had a stale smell that hung around her like a veil. Babcia mumbled. I never heard her utter a real word. I never knew if she was nasty or nice. She was a round stuffed doll, dressed in black, with a funny hairdo. I held my breath when I was forced to be near her or to plant a kiss on her lifeless cheek. Every day my aunt, *Ciocia* Lelia, massaged Babcia with some kind of little buzzing machine. "There, there, Mama," she soothed. "It's getting better." There was another aunt who had gray hair and a teenaged son. People whispered about her husband who had run away.

I liked the pungent, thick smells of the beer hall. I thought the round coasters that were placed under the steins were pretty. They had pictures of Polish kings and names of beers. They were used over and over again. The smell of old ale lived in them permanently. There was a cellar under the beer hall. When it was hot outside, it was nice there. All alone, away from Niania, without my brother, whenever I could, I sneaked down the rickety wooden stairs and disappeared into the dank coolness. I inhaled the special moist smell of the earth and counted the bottles that gleamed in their wooden crates.

The muddy river often overflowed, turning the meadow behind the house into a swamp. When the water level was normal, when it stayed between the riverbanks, Niania sometimes took us to the water's edge to play with our pails. We used them to scoop up tiny fish. We wanted to keep them, to play with them. But in no time all the little fish died, turning sick white bellies toward us.

Chickens pecked in the yard. Sometimes my cousin, who was about twelve, chased one. When he caught the flapping, squawking chicken, he grabbed it by the legs and held it down on a wooden stump. With one blow of an ax he chopped its head off. The headless chicken kept hopping around for a while. Then it stopped and lay completely still. Drops of blood from the chicken's neck trailed him when he carried it to the kitchen.

A tired cow stayed in the meadow even when it got muddy. There she stood, still as a statue, only now and then flicking her tail. A goat was tied to a stick in the yard. I stayed out of its roped-in circle.

I liked picking flowers. Niania taught me how to weave wreaths for my hair. And I liked the wild strawberries we picked in the meadows and the woods. I liked the feeling of the cup or basket getting heavier when I dropped the berries in one by one, all the way up to the rim.

Some days there were farmers' markets on the square. Everywhere there were pigs and sheep. There

were great big cabbages and beets and huge bar-
rels filled with pungent-smelling cucumbers. And
sunflowers. I loved the sunflower disks, heavy and
promising, full of succulent seeds. There were ham-
mered pots and pans made of shiny tin. There were
displays of carved wooden toys. Once, when I was
very little, Niania had bought me one. It was a disk
with chickens. It had a ball on a string that hung
under the disk and a handle. I rotated the handle, and
the chickens pecked, pecked, pecked. I thought it was
such a funny toy. But my chicken toy had not come
with me from Kraków.

On special saints' days there was sometimes a
procession through the village square. Little girls,
throwing flower petals, walked ahead of the priest.
The priest, wearing long robes, sprinkled holy water.
A statue of the Madonna or a saint was carried on
a platform. After the mass in church there was a
dance in the square. The accordion player struck up a
mazurek or a *krakowiak*. The boys kicked their heels.
The girls twirled. I loved the girls' costumes. Their
skirts full and brightly printed with red and pink
roses and green leaves. Their lacy white blouses with
full sleeves. They wore vests embroidered with span-
gles that almost blinded when they sparkled in the
sun. Clumps of ribbons streamed from their shoulders and caught the air.

Even before the war I had felt left outside, only looking in on these celebrations. They were Catholic; they were Polish festivals. A Jewish girl did not belong in their circle.

Living in Łapanów now was not so different from the summers before the Nazis came. Except that now there was no set end to our stay. I missed the city.

Toward the end of the summer in the second year of the war, the skin on my legs became covered with a terrible rash. It began with small red dots that grew into puffy boils that filled with a milky white liquid. "I told you not to pick those mushrooms." Niania was very angry with me. Why she thought that picking mushrooms would give me boils, I don't know. Somebody in the kitchen did cook them, but I never ate any. Being covered with boils was all my fault. Niania kept powdering my legs with white flour from a burlap sack. Or I would be made to soak my legs in a bucket fitted with lukewarm water. I couldn't resist poking holes in the center of the boils. The white liquid ran and left a shriveled flap of skin. I itched. I was stuck with this condition long into the fall. I was so ashamed.

Fall came, and with it endless gray days. It rained and rained. When a Saint's Day procession came by, the statue of the Virgin was covered with a piece of burlap. I caught a glimpse, under dark shawls and coats, of the ribbons and costumes. Later there was no accordion music and no dancing in the square. The market came to town again. People hovered under pieces of cardboard and rags. Niania said that Mother was coming to bring us some money. All day long we sat by the window, looking at the dreary market where we could buy nothing. Waiting and waiting for Mother to arrive. She didn't. I didn't think to worry about her. I just wanted her to bring us some money.

Niania had one of her headaches. We brought her headache powders. The powder was wrapped in squares of wax paper and folded in tiny envelopes each with a picture of a rooster. The powders were called *Kogutki* (Little Roosters). Niania fell asleep. My brother and I sneaked out and wandered between the sad-looking farmers in their stalls. Wilted cabbages and beets dropped from the tables. We found an apple under one of the stands, ran back to the house, and ate it.

When the first snows began to fall, Niania heard news from her village that her mother was sick.

"I want to go to my mother," she cried and cried. "And I can't leave you!" Niania was angry. "Why am I stuck here with you Jews?" Immediately regretting what she had said, she grabbed us, hugged us fiercely, and covered us with kisses. "Poor little children. Poor, poor little children. May the Holy Mother protect you."

One morning Niania woke up shaking, crying. In a dream her mother had been calling to her. "Come, come," Niania's mother had moaned, her hand reaching up from a freshly dug hole in the earth. "My mother grabbed my hand!" Niania whispered. "She kept pulling and pulling." Niania knew this was a bad sign. "My mother was calling to me from her grave. I am so frightened." Soon after Niania had that dream, news came that her mother had died.

Again Niania was angry for being stuck with us. It was all our fault that she couldn't go to her mother's funeral. It was the fault of us Jews.

At last Mother came to Łapanów. She brought some money. By selling her things on the black market, she was surviving in Kraków. So far Mother's papers had kept her safe. Two uncles and their wives had been deported. The Jews still left in the city were in the ghetto now. Uncle Samuel and Aunt Bella and Cousin Raisa were living there. No one had heard from Father.

Now the Łapanów relatives were no longer allowed to run their beer hall. Polish farmers were in charge of serving the Nazi soldiers. *Ciocia* Lena still massaged the old woman with the electric gadget. Niania's headaches were constant. She sat by the window looking at the desolate landscape. She sighed pitifully and cried and cried.

"Are we ever going to see Kraków again?" I asked Niania. As long as I could remember I had liked to think of myself as a girl from the city. Father had left this dreary place so that he could be a well-dressed gentleman wearing cravats and gloves and elegant hats. He had gone away from the muddy fields and his homely relatives. And now he was gone from us. And we were stuck in the place that he had fled from many years ago.

Christmas was coming. "I am too tired to fight your Jewish aunts," Niania grumbled. On Christmas she went to church without us, and we had no tree. "We will have a tree again," she said. "You'll see. By next Christmas the war will be over."

Winter passed. The snow was melting. It was Passover time. Passover celebrations were no longer allowed. *Verboten* was the German word heard over and over again. Forbidden. But the Jewish people in the village were preparing in secret. Matzos had been baked.

Late one evening a Polish man appeared at the house. "They will be going to all the Jewish houses," he warned the relatives. "Be careful."

"You have to be a big, brave girl," *Ciocia* Lelia said

to me in the morning. "You can help us keep our matzos a secret."

Niania was angry. She saw no reason why matzos were so important. Neither did I. "Jews," Niania muttered. *Ciocia* Lelia ignored her.

I had a doll carriage. It was large and deep. *Ciocia* Lelia brought the matzos that had been baked in the night and wrapped in white cloths. She piled them into my doll carriage. We put my dolls on top and covered everything with a heavy blanket. The day was cold and wet. I was bundled up. Heavy felt boots and coat, hat over my ears, and a scarf wrapped around my neck and over my mouth.

I was sent out to walk in the field. Every few steps the doll carriage got stuck, the wheels sinking down deep into the muddy earth. I worried that the carriage would topple over and all the matzos spill out. I tried to be careful. But if I was too careful, it would look suspicious. My woolen scarf itched.

Behind me, at our house, I heard the Germans. They didn't sound dangerous. They just sounded like bullies, who knew they were stronger than the people they were pushing around. I heard them coming closer. I did not stop walking and wheeling the carriage. I even began singing, as if I were a mother rocking her babies to sleep. The two Germans came up behind me.

"*Was hast du da?*" one said, pointing to the carriage. I guessed what he meant.

I smiled at him and answered in Polish, "*To są moje lalki.*" ("Those are my dolls.")

The soldiers were young and handsome. So much better looking than my long-nosed, droopy-eyed cousin who slaughtered chickens. So much better looking than the short, sweaty man with the black cap perched on top of his kinky hair who sometimes came to visit homely *Ciocia* Lelia. But I couldn't think of the Germans as real people. I couldn't separate them from their uniforms and their black-gloved hands and their guns.

The Nazi who had asked me what I had in the carriage was reaching one gloved hand toward me. Any second he would be poking under the blanket. With his hand. With his rifle. They would find the matzos! What would they do to me?

The soldier was smiling, his extended hand hovering in midair. He seemed to want to pat me on the head. The other Nazi adjusted the strap of his rifle and just turned away. The first soldier let his gloved hand drop down by his side. He followed his companion through the field to the next suspected Jewish house.

Did they really believe me? Why would a seven-year-old girl be wandering around, pretending to have a pleasant stroll, pushing a doll carriage through a muddy field?

I kept walking back and forth until Niania came to get me. She hurried me and my load through a side door back into the house. *Ciocia* Lelia took her secret matzos out of my doll carriage. I didn't care what happened to them next. I was relieved to be rid of them. I was happy to be back with Niania.

It was not long after Passover that we began to hear rumors of roundups in nearby villages, It was just as it had been in Kraków. Niania was worried.

"In no time they'll have the Jews of Łapanów on their deportation lists."

Niania had not been back to her own village for many years. "We will go there," she said. "We can live in the house that my mother has left." There were no Jews in that village.

Still, if anyone were to suspect and inform on us, it was easy enough to find out if this sister and brother were Jews. Only Jewish boys were circumcised. Niania decided that from now on it would be safer for my brother to be dressed as a girl.

I never saw the people from Łapanów again.

4

WE RODE ON THE BUS TO A STOP ON THE outskirts of Kraków. Niania had been in touch with Mother. They decided that it would be safer to meet away from the center of the city. How I wished we could go back to Kraków. Back to our apartment. I even wanted to see the Hasid run by our window again. Where was he now? Where was Tatuś?

Mother was waiting for us at the bus stop. She brought a bundle of linens Niania could use to trade when we needed to. The four of us started to walk toward a nearby train station. Mother would wait with us to say good-bye. Niania and my brother and I were going on the train that would take us to Niania's village.

Ahead of us we saw a group of Nazis going in the

same direction as we were. Mother stopped walking. A look of terror on her face. "Don't stop! Keep walking!" Niania whispered. "Keep walking!" We were on a small, quiet street at the edge of the city. Because the wind could have carried even whispers directly to the ears of the Germans ahead, we did not speak. Niania motioned us to turn toward a narrow alley between two houses. The three of us kept in step with her. The alley came to an end at an empty field.

In the distance we could still see the train station. What we had not seen before, because it had been hidden from our sight by buildings, was the long train of boxcars. We could see a milling crowd of people surrounded by Nazis. Now and then we could hear the barking of dogs. We heard no human voices. People were climbing into the boxcars. From the embankment at the end of our street in Kraków I had seen trains of boxcars going by. "Those are not for people to ride in," Niania had told me. "Cows and pigs and vegetables ride in those trains."

"What is happening?" I asked.

"Shh. Don't talk." Mother was leaning against a wall. "Don't ask."

"It's a transport of Jews," said Niania.

Mother had started to cry. Before the war I thought only children cried. Now grown-ups were always bursting into tears. "Father cried and cried when he kissed you good-bye, Hanusiu," Mother had consoled me, assuring me that he really didn't want to leave. I didn't like to have a picture in my head of Father crying. And I remembered the day shortly after the Nazis had taken over Kraków when Mother had come home and cried about her mother and father and sister. Had they been put on one of those cow-car trains I could see in the distance? Was this deportation?

The buildings in the alley were deserted. Niania leaned against a door, and we sneaked in. We were standing on a dusty wooden floor in a hallway. Doors on each side opened into barren rooms. There was no furniture anywhere. Cobwebs and a flypaper crowded with dead flies hung from the ceiling. A torn poster of a man in evening clothes and slicked-down hair, smoking a cigarette, was falling off one of the cracked, peeling walls. Printed on the poster were the words *Pall Mall* and a bunch of other words I could not read.

We stood by the window and watched the crowd of people in the distance struggling, climbing several at a time, into the openings of the boxcars. It was midafternoon by the time the cattle cars were fully loaded. When no more people were left on the track, I watched the Nazis slide the crossbars across the wooden doors. Then they and their dogs boarded a regular passenger car right behind the locomotive.

The train began to pull out. A tail of smoke lingered in the air after it was gone. At no time during the vigil we kept at the window of the abandoned house had we seen the arrival or departure of a regular train at the station.

"I think we should go now," Niania said. We picked up our few bundles and started to walk. The area around the station was quiet and deserted.

"What if no train comes?" I was tired and hungry. "Can we go back to Kraków?"

"Why can't we stay in that empty house we were in?" my brother said.

"You two keep quiet," Niania snapped. Mother sighed and said nothing.

We were alone in the waiting room. I was hoping that no train would come. That we could just start walking toward Kraków. Then a stationmaster wearing his ordinary cap and uniform came in.

"There will be a train soon," he said, smiling. As if he were simply reassuring two women and children going on a pleasure trip that they had no worries. That they would get to where they wanted to go.

"Occasionally we have a necessary delay in the regular running of trains," the stationmaster went on. "We don't want to get in the way of the official operations. I send a telegraph warning to the conductor of the passenger train on the days the Germans load their transports. Until the cattle trains are dispatched, the conductor slows down or even stops his train completely and waits ten or fifteen kilometers from this station."

"That is very smart." Niania nodded. Mother mumbled something softly. The stationmaster left us and went outside. We didn't say anything to one another.

After a few minutes we heard the train whistle in the distance. Soon I could smell the smoke from the locomotive. I could hear the rails humming and clanking. "I have to say good-bye to you now," Mother said. "I will walk back to Kraków." Hastily we embraced.

As soon as the train came to a stop, Niania gathered up our things. We climbed on. We found an empty compartment. The stationmaster gave the green signal and waved to us. We started to move out of the station. When the train switched to another track to make a turn, I saw Mother. Tiny, tiny in the distance, walking rapidly in the direction of our city.

I was excited about riding on a train. The scratchy brown upholstery of the seat teased my thighs and my calves. At this frightening time, even leaving for a place I had never been, I felt a weight fall away from me when the wheels began to turn. The fears and dangers of the whole day dissolved and flowed into the newly greening branches of trees that leaned on the fading afternoon sky. I looked at my brother's curly blond head on Niania's lap. He looked pretty in a skirt and blouse I used to wear. I rested my forehead against the rattling windowpane. I imagined that the train stood still and that the furrowed fields dotted with cows and sheep were really a continuing roll of pictures projected on the other side of the window. It was getting quite dark. I leaned back.

"We are here!" Niania was shaking my shoulder. I had fallen asleep. It was dark when we got off the train. We were alone at the station. "We have to walk to the house," Niania said. She took the suitcase and one bundle. My brother and I carried the other small bundles. With Niania in the middle, we started walking down a dark road. I didn't want to ask if we had far to go. There was no moon to light our way but the sky was full of stars. I wasn't scared. I wasn't even tired. The air was soft and smelled of summer coming. The darkness wrapped itself around us and made me wish that I could just stay in it safely with Niania and my brother. Until the Germans went away. Until Father came back.

Here and there we passed a house with a dim oil lamp or maybe a candle lighting a window. Most of the houses were dark clumps against flat fields and the dark sky. Could there be Nazis living in any of these houses? It was so quiet. Wherever there were Nazis there was always shouting. We walked for a long time but met no one along the way.

"There is my house," Niania said at last. We could make out a small cottage with a hay roof just ahead of us. Niania gave the door a shove. It wasn't locked. We put our things on the earthen floor. The house smelled like the Łapanów cellar. Niania searched in one of her bundles and brought out two candles and matches. She lit the candles and set them down on the wooden bench I had almost fallen over coming in. There was nothing much in the house. A stool by the hearth. A bed against the wall. Over the bed there was a small wooden cross. And next to it a picture of the Sacred Heart.

"Mama, Mama." Niania started to sob. "I have come back. And you are gone."

My brother and I began to cry with her. I put my arms around Niania. "Don't cry, Nianiusiu! Don't cry. Your mama is in heaven with the angels." I was just saying that because I had heard her say it when she talked about dead Catholics.

We started to settle into the little house with a stone hearth and a dirt floor and a roof made of straw. The bed was covered with a feather bolster. The bed frame was filled with hay where a mattress should have been. It was big enough for all three of us to sleep in.

Niania threw one of the sheets Mother had given her over the hay.

"Let's cook some potatoes," she said. There was a large mound of potatoes under the bed. They must have been left there since Niania's mother's death. Many of them had sprouted. Niania had brought along some cooking pots from our kitchen in Kraków. I didn't know she had them. I had never seen her use them in Łapanów. There the Jewish aunts had done all the cooking. There was some water in a barrel by the stove. Niania poured water into one of the pots. I watched her make a small fire. We picked off the sprouts and dropped the potatoes in the boiling water.

In no time we sat at the table and ate boiled potatoes, skins and all. All three of us stepped outside to go to the outhouse. Then we climbed into the hay bed and covered ourselves with the bolster. I felt safe and slept until long after birds started to sing in the trees outside the house.

5

Niania had been away from her village for several years. Only a few of the women, who came to greet her over the next few days, remembered her.

"Your mother died peacefully," one very old woman said. "May *Matka Boska* [Mother of God], protect her soul." Niania stuck to her story that her husband had been killed by the Nazis. "My husband was dead," she said. "Both girls were very sick. I could not come to Mama's funeral." Niania started to cry again. We were her little daughters. We were frail and needed a lot of care.

My brother and I quickly got used to believing that we were sisters. It was not unlikely that my brother could have been Niania's child. Pretty and blond and small-nosed, he didn't look Semitic. With my dark hair and eyes and prominent nose, I was a little suspect as a purebred Polish child. I don't know if anyone believed Niania was our mother.

The village was so small it didn't even have a church. There weren't many people. No one bothered us. Without Niania my brother and I seldom went farther than the sand lot surrounding the house. When it rained or when Niania didn't want us out of the house, we played among the potatoes under the bed. We loved pretending we were in a cave deep down in the earth. We felt safer and happier than we had for a long time.

Along with the linens, Mother had given Niania some of her jewelry that she had managed to hide away from the Nazis. Niania tucked the jewelry into the seam of her jacket and stitched it up. "I hope I never have to use this," she said. When we needed food, she bartered lacy tablecloths, pillowcases, and fine embroidered handkerchiefs for bread, cabbage, fava beans, and white cheese.

We got used to our wanderings through fields and along country lanes. We got used to Niania's knocking on cottage doors or peeking into barns, asking, "Is there some bread or milk you could let me have for my children?" Or, "Can you spare an egg?" Thinking we were beggars, the peasants often met us with

sour expressions on their faces. When Niania pulled
out a linen towel or table napkins or a pillowcase,
they looked at us differently. The women, especially,
peered with interest at the nice things, once Mother's
prized possessions. I didn't care about these things.
I don't know if Niania did. She was just glad when
milk was poured into our small tin bucket, or she was
handed a loaf of bread or some beans in a scrap of rag
in exchange for her offerings.

Once an old, old woman got so excited about an
embroidered tablecloth that she invited us in. "Come,
come," she said. "Sit down." At first Niania tried to
protest. Mostly because she was surprised. On our
trading walks no one had ever invited us into a house
before. Then she decided it was all right. We stepped
inside a cottage that was even smaller than Niania's.
The woman unfolded the tablecloth from our dining
room in Kraków and laid it on her little shaky wooden
table by the window. The tablecloth was huge. It hung
down in great folds, fanning out, covering a large part
of the earthen floor in the tiny cottage.

"It is beautiful," the old woman sighed. "I remember . . . I remember such lovely things." When she
was younger, she had been a maid at the house of
pani Ziemiańska in Warszawa (Warsaw). "I washed
and ironed all the table linens," she said. "I always
knew by the stains what the family and guests had

been served for dinner the night before." Then the old woman offered us what was left of a poppy-seed cake she had baked. We sat at the table with the cloth billowing over our laps and legs, each of us nibbling a slice of the *makownik*. We were careful not to spill the little black seeds. Touching and smoothing out her new tablecloth, the old woman smiled at my brother and me and said to Niania, "What nice daughters you have."

I looked at the garlands of delicate white flower embroidery. "I remember this tablecloth from the Sed—" I started to say.

"Sch, don't interrupt," Niania said quickly. She tried to sound like a mother politely disciplining her child. "Can't you see that the lady is talking to me?" The old woman chattered on to Niania about her servant days.

With the delicious taste of *makownik* on my tongue, I had forgotten myself. The Seder! I had almost said. The Seder! The old woman went on and on about *pani* Ziemiańska. My brother went on slowly eating his slice of cake. I knew he was trying to make it last. Before the visit ended, the woman cried about the memories of her life before the Nazis came. "Those were good times." She sighed. "Good times."

It was almost evening when we said good-bye to the nice old woman. She gave us a big loaf of brown bread, a head of cabbage, and some cucumbers. She went to her chicken coop and gave us the eggs that her hens had laid that morning. "Please come again," she said to Niania. "May the Christ Child bless and protect your little girls." She stood outside her cottage and watched us walk away across the fields. We kept looking back and waving until we could no longer see either the woman or her house.

One hot day, after we had walked for a long time along a dusty road, we came tired and hungry to a cottage. A cow was grazing in a field nearby. Maybe we can get some milk, I thought. Before Niania even had a chance to knock, a large peasant woman blocked the door.

"Could I exchange this for a loaf of bread and milk for my children?" Niania pulled a linen sheet out of the bundle she was carrying. She unfolded it, skillfully hanging it over one arm. The woman glared suspiciously at all three of us. Behind the older woman a younger fat blond woman stood holding a naked baby boy. The two women began to paw the sheet. They stuck their thick fingers into the rest of Niania's linen bundle, leaving greasy marks. The young woman snatched a folded handkerchief and held it up to her nose. The baby grabbed for it. She slapped his hand and snatched the handkerchief from him. He began to scream. She went back into the house. The older woman took the sheet and followed her.

She came back with a knife in her hand and a large loaf of bread. She held the circular loaf sideways against her heavy bosom, and in a quick, clean motion, sliced the bread in half.

"Take this," the woman said to Niania, handing her half of the round loaf of bread.

The fat young woman came back carrying some white cheese still dripping in a cloth. "Here," she said. "Take this, too." Niania thanked them. My brother and I curtsied.

We walked away alongside the house. By the open upper window I saw the fat young woman, now without the baby, holding a chamber pot. When we passed the window, she leaned out over the ledge and emptied the chamber pot on our heads.

Urine trickled down my face. Feces stuck to my cheeks and hair. My brother was equally covered. The slop wasn't from the baby. It was grown-up stuff. I could tell. While the older woman had been cutting the bread, the younger woman had time to sit on the pot. Why did she do this? Wasn't the handkerchief she picked out nice enough? And they had given us food! And then I thought: They guessed—they guessed we were Jews.

They could smell us on the handkerchief, the sheet!

"They must know. They guessed!" I whispered. "Nianiusiu! They know!" Behind us a dog barked. I grabbed my brother's hand and started to run.

"Don't run!" Niania stopped us. "Don't be frightened! They are just filthy peasants. I know their kind."

Maybe she did. She came from this village. Maybe she knew what the peasants from this part of the country did to strangers. Even those they didn't suspect of being Jews.

We obeyed Niania. Steadily all three of us started to walk back across the field. The cow turned her head and mooed. I was usually scared of cows. Now I didn't care if she followed us. The cow went back to her chewing.

The day was hot. Through the stinking contents of the chamber pot drying on my skin, I could smell the fresh bread in Niania's bundle. I was hungry. Only a few drops of the chamber pot shower seemed to have dripped on Niania. The food was safe. We came to a grove of trees and some shade. There was a brook and clear, clean water. Alone, the three of us took off most of our clothes and washed ourselves. Niania rinsed our clothes and laid everything out to dry in the sun. She checked the bundle of linen. It was clean.

We tore off pieces of the black bread and smeared the white cheese on it with a small knife Niania carried in her bundle. She carried tin cups, too. We filled them with water from the brook. Everything tasted so good. The sun was shining. It was good not to be hungry. On the way back to our village we picked cornflowers and poppies growing in the wheat fields.

Niania had her usual headaches. "I want to go to church," she complained, "but I don't want to go with you two."

We trudge around to houses to get food, I thought. Why can't we walk to the church in the next village? "I would like to go to church, too!"

"People come to mass from all over this area," Niania said. "Who knows what suspicions could start if I parade you around in church?" It was because of me. I was dark. I had a big nose. I looked more Jewish than my brother. It was all my fault.

Yet these were not bad times. I often almost forgot the dangers that we had left behind, far away, in the city. We continued our wanderings in search of milk and bread and cheese. Sometimes we got some butter and even *kiełbasa* (sausage). And there were always potatoes to eat. In late summer we could get ripe heads of sunflowers. I loved the weight of the large disk. We poked our fingers into the crown and picked the seeds out of their pockets. I loved to crack the shell between my teeth. I loved the moment after the shell was spit out. What remained was the delicate seed of the sunflower to nibble on.

My brother and I found a little gray kitten and brought him back to the house. Niania didn't want us to keep him. She thought cats carried evil spells within them. My brother and I loved the little cat. We called him Duszek. Among the potatoes under our bed we made a little straw bed for Duszek. Niania persisted in trying to take the cat away from us. One day she chased Duszek with a broomstick and slammed the door on him. I heard a small, piercing cry and a sound, like that of a breaking twig. One of Duszek's front legs had been caught in the door and broken. My brother and I tried to fix it. We wrapped a rag soaked in water around Duszek's little leg. He meowed and limped around outside for a while. And then he was gone. My brother and I searched everywhere, but Duszek had limped away forever. I don't know if Niania was sorry. I know that she didn't believe that the Virgin bothered protecting animals.

One night we were wakened by terrible shouting in the village. We looked through the window and saw men holding pitchforks, running down the road. "*Boże mój!* [My God!] Get under the bed! Quick!" Niania was sure they were coming for us. "Someone informed." We scurried under the bed and made ourselves small among the potatoes. "If they want to find us, they will," my brother whispered. The men ran right by our house.

As soon as we knew that the commotion didn't have anything to do with us, we crept to the window. In the moonlight we saw a young man standing in the middle of the road surrounded by the men with pitchforks. An older man and woman were shaking their fists at him and screaming. They were holding back a young woman who was trying to push through the screaming and gesticulating circle of people to the man who was being attacked. We couldn't hear what they were shouting about.

We knew these people. The pretty young woman had been nice to my brother and me. She had tried to help us look for Duszek. Niania was relieved that none of this had anything to do with us. "Vodka," she muttered. "They are all drunks." She herded us back to the bed. "Let them have their fights," she said. "They won't have time to think about us."

A few days later there were festivities in the village. There was to be a wedding. We were invited. "We can't go." Niania didn't want us to be stared at. She told the village people that my sister and I were sick. The bride came to our cottage before the wedding to show us her dress. It was made of shiny blue material sprinkled with cornflowers. She had long blond braids and wore a wreath of field flowers in her hair. I gave her a bouquet of flowers I had picked. Niania said I should fall on my knees before her and sing a song. I felt as if I were in church and the Virgin had come to life. I sang the bride a well-known song about a *Krakowianka,* a poor girl from Kraków, and her loved one. I had learned the song when I was very little.

Out of our window we watched the wedding procession on its way to church. The bride and the man who had been threatened with pitchforks a few nights earlier were riding in a wagon pulled by two horses. The wagon had been decorated with flowers. The bridegroom had a white shirt under his embroidered vest and a Polish soldier's *kepi* on his head.

"If there were Nazis around," Niania said, "he would not have dared to put that cap on his head." Then why didn't she let us go to the wedding? I wanted so much to be in church and sing and see the bride and groom at the altar.

Later I heard Niania talking with some of the village women. "Did you see the stomach on her?" said one, and crossed herself. Another rolled her eyes and clucked her tongue. I didn't understand. I thought the bride was the most beautiful girl I had ever seen. And I wished I had long blond braids and a blue dress with flowers.

6

THEN UNEXPECTEDLY MOTHER APPEARED. THE
Nazis had emptied out all the things in our apartment.
All Jewish apartments in Kraków had been confiscated. Uncle, Aunt, and Cousin Raisa had long since
been taken to the ghetto. With her false identity papers,
Mother had managed to stay out. But now she felt she
might be safer in the country. Of the linens, gloves, and
pocketbooks she had used to trade on the black market,
very little was left.

"I have nothing! Nothing," Mother cried. "And I
want to be with you."

We weren't exactly hiding. But Niania had tried to
keep us quietly out of sight. She had kept to her story
that her two girls were frail children and needed constant watching. No one had bothered us. Mother's

arrival changed all that. I looked very much like my mother. I was marked. No longer would anyone believe that I was Niania's child.

A man I had never seen in the village before began to come to the house and have whispered conversations with Mother. From among the potatoes under the bed, my brother and I peeked and listened. "*Pani* should be warned," the man was saying. "It is easy for anyone to go to the nearest Nazi headquarters, and suggest that there are Jews hiding in the area."

"Everyone knows those little girls are mine!" we heard Niania say. The man laughed.

Mother brought out her identity papers. He waved them away. "I can be of help," he said. "I will come back later." It was clear that he was ready to inform on us if he wanted to.

"*Pani* should not have come here." Niania was angry at Mother! "If *pani* had stayed away, the children would have been safe."

Later that afternoon the man came back. My brother and I watched from under the bed as my mother took a sparkling brooch and a pearl necklace from a small pouch hanging on a string around her neck and pressed these pieces of jewelry into the man's hands. Mother then said good-bye to us and left with the man. Niania told us that we, too, had to get ready to leave.

The same evening, when it had begun to get dark,

the man came back with a horse and hay wagon. "I took her to the train station this afternoon," the man said. "*Pani* has left." We put our bundles together and climbed under the hay. If people in the village knew what was going on, they said nothing. Either they were nice or they didn't care. Hidden under the hay, we had no way of knowing where the man was taking us. We bumped along a road, not daring to peek out, for a long time. Finally we heard the man say, "Brrrrr," to his horse. The wagon came to a halt. Out we climbed. We found ourselves in front of the same train station that we had arrived at months ago. It looked deserted.

"There will be a train to Kraków soon," the man said. He got back onto his hay wagon and rode away.

I was scared. But once again I was excited about riding a train. And we were going back to the city. Back to Kraków. My brother looked sleepy. Niania looked stern.

Mother was gone. I hadn't thought much about her. She had come and created a stir. That was why we were on the run again.

It was true that the man who had brought us to the train station had been properly bribed. But he could easily have accepted Mother's jewelry and lied to us about taking her to the train to Kraków. He might have been scared that the Nazis would find out what he knew, and just to be on the safe side, he could have gone to a local headquarters. With every passing moment I expected Nazis to burst in through the door.

Time dragged for us in the empty station. We couldn't really be sure that a train would come. Then some women carrying bundles and a man with a black band tied over one eye walked in. I didn't recognize anyone from our village. It would have been better to be alone, avoiding the stares of the peasants who sat with us in the waiting room. At least the arrival of the other people was a sign that there would be a train. I could tell Niania was very nervous because she snapped, "Sit still, Hanusiu." She was always trying to make sure that we stayed unnoticed.

"I am sitting still," I whispered. Couldn't she see that? I listened impatiently for the promise of knocking in the rails.

It was late at night when we heard the train whistle in the distance. A sleepy stationmaster came out of his little cubicle, holding his signal sign. He held up the green side. The train puffed and clanked into the station. We climbed the steps onto the train. A cloud of white and gray smoke wrapped us. I wished it would wrap itself around us like a feather bolster and hide us from sight. We found seats. The train was not crowded. Still, I felt surrounded by suspicious looks. I saw potential informers who could instantly see that I was Jewish everywhere. My brother fell asleep.

When the wheels began to roll on the rails at last, I begged Niania to let me stick my head out of the window. In the night wind and in the sulfuric coal smoke whipping my face I found the veil I had been looking for ever since my mother had appeared in the village. I shut my eyes so the cinders from the smoke would not fly in. The sound of the wheels rhythmically passing over the joints in the rails made me feel that I was part of a wonderful adventure. Just being on a journey felt like freedom.

Back in Kraków we went to see Uncle Samuel's and Aunt Bella's maid, Jadwiga. She had stayed in their old apartment. A Nazi family was living there now. They had kept Jadwiga in their service. She was alone when we got there. "The German family has gone to the country for a few days," she said. We found out from Jadwiga that Mother had come back safely. The man in the village had taken her jewelry and kept his word.

"*Pani* decided to sneak into the ghetto for now," Jadwiga said. "It was the only thing she could do. And she wanted to see her brother." All the rest of Mother's family had been deported. Uncle Samuel and his wife and daughter were the only ones left.

"*Pani* thinks the children have to go to her," Jadwiga said then. I didn't understand what she was talking about. "*Boże mój!* I am helpless." Niania was wringing her hands. Now that staying with Jadwiga was out of the question, Niania cried, "We have nowhere to go!" Finally she agreed with Jadwiga. My brother and I had to go to the ghetto.

"Things are quiet there right now," Jadwiga said. "There have been no rumors of deportation." She knew of a secluded spot where two children could easily slip in without being noticed. "And I have ways to stay in touch."

All this was crazy! We had been safe enough in Niania's village until Mother showed up. Why did she come back to Kraków just to go to the ghetto?

"I don't want to go away from you!" I was crying and hugging my *niania*. Jadwiga was working for Nazis. Why did Niania believe everything she was saying?

"I promise, Hanusiu!" Niania crossed herself. "I will not abandon you! I swear on the Sacred Heart that I will come for you." As soon as she found a safe place for us to stay, she would come. She hugged my brother and me. She blessed us. If Niania swore on the holy image, she had to keep her promise. I had to trust her. "I will not abandon you," Niania repeated. I calmed down. My brother didn't cry, didn't say anything.

Guards did not always bother watching every point of the segregated part of the city. Jadwiga's dark alley between two buildings wasn't guarded by the usual pair of Germans parading back and forth with their rifles. My brother and I easily walked in. We didn't see anyone. We held hands and looked straight ahead. We didn't walk too fast, trying to keep our steps quiet on the cobblestones. We didn't talk. We walked through a dark passage. We came to the center of an open square. In an iron fountain water trickled out of the tongue of a grotesque, contorted face. The sun was shining. It was warm. We were alone.

It was the first time that my brother and I had been in this place where the Kraków Jews had been herded the first year of the war. Until now *ghetto* had been only a word to us. It did not feel like a prison. Just a muffled place in a secluded part of the city.

I was surprised to see Mother. When she left with the Polish man in Niania's village, I am not sure that I thought much about whether I would see her again. There she stood now on the corner dressed in an old familiar suit and hat she used to wear to the office before the Nazis had come. She stood still. Not making a move toward us. The sun, sparkling on the steel fitting of the handbag she was clutching, seemed noisy. But there were no sounds anywhere. And no people. No Jews. No Nazis. No one.

7

MOTHER INSTALLED US IN HER CORNER OF THE apartment she was sharing with Uncle Samuel and Aunt Bella and Cousin Raisa. There was a bed for all three of us to sleep in. Some suitcases and bundles were stuffed under the bed. We might have walked into a waiting room in a railroad station once again. Uncle and Aunt and Cousin Raisa had lived like this ever since the Nazis took over all the Jewish properties and apartments in Kraków. *Confiscated.* I had already added that word to the others in my war vocabulary. Climbing the stairs to the fourth floor, I had smelled cabbage soup cooking. Things to cook must have been found somewhere. I was hungry. We ate stale bread spread with a dark red, sweet marmalade and drank water. I thought of all the potatoes we had left under the bed in the country.

I hadn't seen my cousin Raisa since before my brother and I had left with Niania for Łapanów. When the Germans had taken over the city, she was fourteen years old. Shortly before the war I had watched my cousin, with the girls in her school class, marching in a parade. The sun was shining, but Raisa wore a raincoat of a transparent material that a relative had just sent her from America. The raincoat covered her from the neck to below her knees. It had a hood that she had put over her head. She looked like a doll in a cellophane wrapping. I could see her braids hanging down her back and everything she wore. The pleated skirt. The blazer of her school uniform. She wore white knee socks and grown-up shoes that didn't have to be laced up to the ankles like mine. She laughed and was prettier and stood out from the other girls. She was magical. I wanted to have a transparent raincoat and march in a parade. I wanted to go to school and have friends and play "Für Elise" on the piano. Just like Raisa.

Raisa had had to stop going to school. And my brother and I had never gone. Only Polish kids who promised to be just like the German Hitler Youth were allowed to go to school and to march in parades. I had seen them on the streets of Kraków before we had fled to Łapanów. They wore dark shirts with neat kerchiefs around the necks. They lifted their legs in unison. They saluted with outstretched arms, just like soldiers.

They were on the right side of things. I wished I could be on the right side of things. Away from Jews. And now we were in the ghetto.

When Raisa and her parents were sent to the ghetto, their piano had been confiscated. I wondered what had happened to the transparent raincoat. Raisa didn't look as nice as she used to. The thick, long braids that had hung down her back or had been coiled around her ears were gone.

"Did the Germans cut your hair?" I asked.

"I cut the hair off myself," Raisa snapped. "There is no shampoo powder to keep it clean."

As the war went on, we were no longer able to find the flat navy blue envelopes of powder that had pictures of very pretty ladies on them. Diagonally across the shampoo packets the model posed, one leg in the air, a high-heeled shoe dangling from her toes. Her neck was bent back and her long, shiny, wavy black or light brown or blond hair hung down. Niania used to buy the blond shampoo for herself and my brother, the black for me. For a long time now we had washed our hair with coarse soap, if we could find even that. Or we just sloshed our hair around in a bucket of water. And we could never quite get rid of the lice. Just when we thought that we had managed to explode the last bug by pressing the nails of our thumbs together, Niania found more white dots that looked like the tiniest of rosary beads clinging here and there to a strand of hair on all our heads.

Through the iron grille of the balcony in the ghetto apartment, we looked down on a courtyard paved with cobblestones. The German guards usually walked back and forth in pairs. As if that were safer for them. Laughing. Almost not a threat to anyone. When a Jewish person walked out, he or she walked looking straight ahead, uncomfortable without the shelter of a wall, a door, anything to slip behind. Just as when my brother and I, sneaking in, had wanted to disappear into some magic covering that would make us invisible.

We were always told to be very quiet. The whispers of the trapped grown-ups sounded like the noise of insects rubbing their legs together. Below us, above us, we felt the hushed lives of caged people. Waiting for something to change. Praying for rescuers. Even dreaming that the Nazis would lose interest, yawn, and go away.

It was another warm September. The sky above the courtyard was cloudless. Somewhere the end of summer must have been beautiful and real. In the ghetto rumors about liquidation were growing. That led to roundups and transports. Didn't it? And deportation on cattle trains? No one had mentioned Niania since we had entered. My brother and I sat in the corner by the bed and whispered.

"Do you think she'll come?" my brother asked.

"Of course she will," I told him. Around our necks hung the medals of the Virgin and the Christ Child, St. Anthony, and other saints that Niania trusted. The relatives had shaken their heads and tried to take the medals away from us. I wouldn't let them.

It was when the war began and we had really become her children that Niania had hung the medals around our necks. I loved to caress my medals. With my finger I followed the outline of the little, raised figure of the Virgin, hands outstretched, standing on the globe. I could feel the tiny dots that were supposed to be stars on the halo above her head. Whenever I touched my medals, I felt safer. The medals made us less Jewish. The Holy Mother and Niania would take care of us again.

And then came the moment when we were once again shaken from our suspended time and were forced to think of hiding or running.

"It will start in the morning." A man was speaking to my uncle at the door. "Be ready," he whispered. "I'll be back."

Everything was quiet. We waited. All night my brother and I sat on the floor in a corner of the room and waited silently in the dark. Voices and sounds from the other apartments below and above faded and transformed into the uncertain scratchings of mice. Now and then the silence was pierced by the rumblings of a truck or a siren from far away in the free part of the city. I don't know if I dozed off.

There was a quick rapping on the door. The man who had talked to Uncle the night before was back. He was tall and not very dark. He didn't look Jewish. "Come with me." He motioned to my mother and my brother and me.

We knew that there were healthy Jewish men who had been forced by the Nazis to help root out people who might try to escape. If he was one of them, why did he risk trying to help us? My uncle had been a successful architect. Maybe the man had worked for him. Maybe that was it. Where was he taking us? Why should we trust him?

"Go with him!" Uncle said. "He knows what to do!"

"You stay here and wait," the man said to my uncle and aunt and cousin Raisa. "I'll be back."

My brother and I followed Mother and the man as quietly as we could up a flight of stairs.

Beyond the top floor and above the attic there was a narrow space. It was packed with men and women lying side by side on the floor right under the beams of the sloping roof. The smell of sweaty bodies and moth-balls blended with the summery country smell of dry wood and dust. I held my nose. The hiding place was stifling. "They can't come in here," I heard a woman whisper. "We can't allow three more people!"

Two Hasidic Jews in long black coats and curls by their ears grumbled, *"Kinder!* [Children!] Don't bring *Kinder* in here! They won't keep still." I remembered Niania's dislike of the Hasid at home on our balcony. "The *Kinder* will give us away."

"Be quiet!" Our man was angry. "You have to let them in! Or I'll add you to the list!" That took care of the complaining.

We crept on all fours through the low opening. One Hasid moved over to make a space for Mother. My brother climbed over her and fitted himself in. I slipped into what space there was by her other side. "No one make a sound," the man who brought us said. "And don't anyone make the slightest move until I come back." He shut the low door behind him and was gone, leaving a frightened, resentful heap of bodies suspended, not daring to stir or hardly breathe. Only some boards and a thin layer of crumbling plaster separated us from the apartment below.

We lay there. A bunch of smelly Jewish strangers. For hours we were like the contents of a boiling pot on the stove. Waiting for the lid to be lifted and for the stew to be ladled out. And because we had hidden and not waited respectfully for the roundup, the Nazis would surely take us out to the courtyard, line us up, and shoot us at once. Niania had always been so smart about knowing where to go. Why had we been brought to this? Why was Niania allowing this to happen to us? Walking from house to house in the country, trading sheets for bread and potatoes, had been fun. Running and hiding from the peasants had been better than this.

All day we lay there listening to the German voices. In the distance at first. Shouting and swearing their usual: *"Raus. Schnell. Verfluchte, schmutzige Juden."* ("Out. Quick. Damned, filthy Jews.") They were coming closer and closer until there was no doubt that they had arrived at our building. No complaints were heard from the people being flushed out. Only the sounds of bundles scraping on the stairs. The thud of a dropped parcel, the erupting anger of the impatient Germans hurrying people along. In the midst of this hive of silent madness, in our space under the roof I had a realization that reached beyond the terror and discomfort of my own body. I heard no cries of babies! No children's footsteps. Where were they? Were there no more children?

At last the Germans reached the top apartment of the building. If anyone among us had sneezed or if a plank had squeaked, Nazi rifles would have crashed through the low walls and the ceiling.

I felt an itch on my head. I didn't dare lift my hand

to scratch for fear of banging into one of the beams. I moved my eyes without moving my head and looked at my mother. So still. Lying flat on her back. Her eyes were open, but she looked like the corpse of an old woman we had known in the country. The dead woman had been laid out on a table in her cottage. Her nose, long and thin, reached far away from her face. And her feet were neatly pointing straight up. Mother's big nose and pointing feet looked just like that corpse.

My eyes caught a glimpse of my brother. He was such a pretty girl and so obedient. He didn't let his eyes roll. He kept them closed. Maybe he had fallen asleep.

By the time the noises of the raid subsided, an eternity had passed. It must be evening now, I thought. I felt the darkness rather than saw it. People began to stir. "Sch," my mother hissed. "Don't move yet." We heard steps coming toward the entrance of our hiding place. It could still have been a Nazi making a last check. But it was the man who had brought us here. He motioned to us from the low, narrow opening to the attic. We could leave.

I tried to move my arms and legs. They were numb. Bracing myself against the floor, I managed to lift myself to a crouch. People were unfolding their limbs. All around in the heavy air, relief and a kind of joy blended with the smells we had produced during hours of lying down in this packing crate.

"It was right here by my side the whole time!" I heard Mother whisper angrily to the Hasid who had not wanted to let us in. "Now it's gone!" Mother had had a small purse with some money in it. It was the only thing she had carried with her to the hiding place. Now it was missing. Under the low roof Mother and the Hasid were facing each other on their knees. She grabbed him and began to shake him by the shoulders. "Did you take it, you swine?" He pushed Mother aside. Muttering something, he crept away. The rest of the people had started to crawl on hands and knees toward the opening of the attic. Uncertainly, quietly, all of us began making our way down the stairs.

The man who had helped us took us back to Uncle and Aunt and Raisa. They had remained safely in the apartment. The man must have known that they were not on the list. Officially Mother and my brother and I would not have been on any list. We had sneaked in. We had walked into the ghetto without permission. That would have made things even worse for us with the Nazis. Uncle Samuel and the man who saved us embraced.

Mother cried about her lost purse. "How can a Jew do such a thing?" How could she get so upset about a little purse? I was glad to have my body back. Glad that the Nazis had left. That for now I didn't have to think about their rifles crashing through the wall.

Mother was embracing what was left of her family. *"Gott sei Dank* [Thank God]," Uncle Samuel said. For the moment we were safe. With my brother I sat in a corner exhausted and stunned. We had survived a real Nazi raid. Now what?

I don't know how he knew, but a few days later Uncle said that a good unguarded spot had been found. My brother and I could sneak out of the ghetto and go back to Niania.

8

IN BROAD DAYLIGHT ON AN AUTUMN DAY MY brother and I set out to cross a small stone bridge out of the ghetto. The day was warm and still. There was sunshine and a blue sky. The bridge was bordered on both sides by a balustrade of short columns. Slightly ahead of us we could see the heads and shoulders of two German guards. Laughter and the smell of their cigarettes drifted toward us. I could see the bayonets on the tops of their rifles peeking up. Walking as we did down the middle of the bridge, I hoped that we were hidden from view. Under our feet this short, solid stone walkway felt like a tightrope. I held my brother's hand. We will get across, I thought. We will. We had squeaked by in other situations. This was just another adventure. Already, with every step, the distance to the safe side was shrinking. The guards were not looking in our direction. Not yet.

And then we saw Niania. She stood leaning in the doorway of the first building on the other side of the bridge. She held a string bag in her hand. How smart Niania is, I thought. She is pretending to be a lady just stepping out of her house and going to market. I could tell that my brother wanted to run to her. I squeezed his hand so hard that he just put one foot in front of the other and kept pace with me. We were about halfway to the other side when a motorcycle driven by a Nazi, with another Nazi in the sidecar, rumbled onto the bridge. They came to a stop ahead of us and shouted something to the soldiers under the bridge. Any second now they would have to see us. I felt my brother's grip tighten on my hand.

I thought of the beautiful angel in the picture that had hung over our bed before the war. Her giant wings hovering over, almost enveloping two children crossing a bridge over a ravine. Please make my brother and me invisible. There are only a few more steps to take, and we will be with Niania, I thought. I prayed that Niania would just stand still in her doorway. We would get across. We had to. I heard the motor start again. We kept on walking. The motorcycle with the two Nazis drove away in the direction it had come from. The other two soldiers were now hidden from our sight under the bridge. We walked almost directly over their heads, still hearing their voices. As we reached Niania in her doorway, I could still smell the smoke from their cigarettes. The soldiers had not bothered to notice two children quietly walking over a bridge.

Niania's lips were closed tight. Her face was still as a mask. She looped the string bag around her arm and took my brother's hand. Then she took my hand. With Niania in the middle, slowly, as if we were deliberately measuring the stones on the sidewalk with our feet, we walked away from the ghetto.

9

WHEN NIANIA CAME FOR US AT THE GHETTO bridge, she had brought with her a piece of black cloth. As soon as we were out of danger, she made a makeshift bandage and wrapped it around my head, covering my right eye. "I have found a place to stay," Niania said. "We will be safe." She had found a shelter at a convent of Benedictine sisters. The hospital across the street from the convent was run by the brothers of the same order. We needed to stay at the shelter so that I could see a doctor. I needed treatment for my eye, was the story Niania had told the nuns. I don't know what else she told them. The Benedictines let us in.

Niania had devised the eye condition not only to get us in but also to hide part of my face from the world. To hide one of my heavy-lidded dark eyes that looked sadly Semitic. Every time I looked at myself in the mirror all I could think was: Jew, Jew. Ugly, obvious Jew girl. Under his skirt my brother had more incriminating things to hide. But to the outside world he was a small-nosed, pretty blond girl.

The bandage covering my eye was often uncomfortable. It got caught in my eyelashes, the skin itched, and my eye smarted. I never forgot which eye the bandage went over. My lid was getting squashed. My eye really started to look as if it needed medical attention. Sometimes when I thought it was safe and Niania wasn't looking, I pushed the rag up on my forehead. But mostly, from the moment I woke in the morning until I went to sleep at night, I dutifully kept my bandage in place.

We stayed in a large room with other women. There was a similar room for the men. We were so used to my brother's being a girl that we began to believe he really was. If Niania had had to explain anything to the nuns, it wasn't talked about. The three of us stayed together. Not unlike a hospital ward, the room had two neat rows of white beds. We were assigned a corner with two beds made up with clean sheets. My brother and I had one bed and Niania took the other. Everyone was responsible for keeping her area clean. There was a dining hall with wooden tables and benches. The nuns served a vegetable soup with cabbage and beans and potatoes. I thought the soup was delicious. We prayed before and after every meal.

Life in the convent was good. The nuns were nice. We were back in the city that I loved. When we didn't go to the little Benedictine chapel for mass, we went to *kościół Mariacki* (Church of St. Mary), the big church in the main square. Niania was less worried about being seen with us in a large cathedral in the city than she had been in a little village church in the country. When we were not in church, my brother and I often chanted the mass, which we had learned by heart. In our performances we secretly returned my brother to his maleness. In our play my brother was always the celebrant, I the chorus of nuns and the congregation.

In our ward at the convent we made friends with a girl with rosy cheeks. Krysia and her mother had two beds facing ours on the other side of the aisle. "She looks very well," people assured her mother. But our friend was not well. Her flushed red cheeks were a dreaded sign of tuberculosis.

My brother and I had fun with Krysia. We climbed the brick wall that surrounded the courtyard of the convent and walked balancing on top. Krysia teased and pulled my hair.

"Why is your sister's hair short?" she asked. "Her hair is prettier than yours." I got scared. Krysia was smart.

"Curly hair looks nicer when it's short," my brother said quickly. "Mama likes it that way." He could be smart, too.

We sat on the branch of an oak tree that grew in the courtyard, swinging our legs. We could see the river and the Wawel Castle from there.

"Mama says we will not be staying with the sisters much longer." Krysia's mother had told her that they were waiting for Krysia's father, the count. He was coming soon to take them away. "I don't think he is really coming," Krysia said.

Krysia's mother was beautiful. She had blue eyes and blond hair that fell in waves in a way I had seen only on the heads of movie stars. Every evening, in a little tin basin she kept by her bed, she washed a white lace blouse. She squeezed out the water. She smoothed her blouse. Finally she hung it to dry on a string she had tied between Krysia's bed and her own. Every morning she looked over the blouse carefully and sewed up little rips with a needle and thread that she kept in a small, worn leather suitcase under the bed. The case had elegant brass fittings. I don't know what other things she kept in it. She often rummaged in its contents in search of something. "Go play with your friends, Krysiu," she would say, wanting to be left alone to concentrate on something in her little suitcase.

The Benedictine shelter had one real bathroom on the second floor of the building where most of us lived. It had running water and a sink. And a big bathtub that stood on heavy legs that looked like the paws of lions. We never used this bathroom. We carried the water in a bucket from the well in the yard. Then we filled a big tin bowl with a pitcher. We washed in our own corner. Niania washed our clothes. We had a chamber pot under our bed. We still had lice, but other than that our bodies didn't feel so dirty.

One day my brother and I were running up and down the stairs, playing hide-and-seek. We were searching for Krysia. We passed the bathroom. I tried the door. It was locked. "She must be in there," my brother whispered. I pushed my eyepatch up and looked through the keyhole.

I saw a naked old woman in the tub sunk up to her waist in water. It took me a moment or two even to recognize her. It was Sister Ignacja. The only parts of any nun I had ever seen uncovered had been feet in sandals. Arms were never visible above the elbow, and the face was always framed by starched white and covered with the brown wimple. I saw that Sister Ignacja had a little hair on her head. Just a short gray stubble. I watched the nun soap a rag and carefully wash her flat, thin breasts, which bobbed in the bathwater. She reached down and washed between her legs. I moved away from the keyhole and made my brother take a look. He started to giggle. I put my hand over his mouth and pulled him away from the bathroom door.

Why had this sight been put in our way? I was ashamed, and I was frightened. We had looked at something we had no right to see. Looking at a naked nun was certainly a sin. We had not intended to be sinful. But I had been interested in the sight. If I had been alone, I know I would have taken another good look at old Sister Ignacja to see what she did in her bath.

I hoped that Krysia would not suddenly appear from somewhere. "Let's not look for Krysia anymore," I said to my brother. I was sure she would tell Niania what we had seen. She might even tell the nuns. My brother and I walked quietly down one flight of stairs and sat on a bench in the courtyard.

It was a nice warm day. Several nuns were peeling potatoes under a tree. Now all I could think of was their naked bodies under the brown habits. And shaved heads under the wimples. I didn't want to think of the sisters that way. I thought that the bodies of priests and nuns were excused from many things the rest of us did. If the war ever came to an end, if I could forever stop being Jewish, I wanted to become a nun. I had seen the nuns with rolled-up sleeves washing their hands and arms. Washing dishes. Washing clothes. But I never thought that they had to pee and make and take a rag and wash between their legs. Sitting there in the tub, Sister Ignacja had been so terribly naked.

"We can't tell Niania about this," I said to my brother.

"And we won't tell Krysia either," he decided.

If we had gone to confession, our sin could have been taken away. But that Niania would not allow. We prayed. We sang. We spent hours on our knees in church and in the convent chapel. From the *Kyrie Eleison* to the *Ite Missa est, Deo Gracias*, we knew the mass in Latin by heart. The Holy Mother and the saints would protect us. Niania always told us that. But we were not Catholics. Communion was out of the question. We were Jews. And Jewish sins were worse. Always worse. My brother and I were sitting quietly, hanging on to our secret, when Krysia came running toward us, the two red spots on her cheeks blazing.

"We looked for you everywhere," I lied.

"I was practically waving a flag at you from under the chapel stairs." Krysia was indignant. "Both of you girls must be blind, blind, blind."

10

ONE DAY WE WENT TO MASS AT THE BIG CHURCH on the main square. It was a warm day.

When we left after mass, Niania discovered that she had forgotten her jacket in the pew. We ran back to look for it, but it was gone. We looked in pew after pew. We crawled and looked on the stone floor. We even searched areas that we had not gone near. When we asked the sacristan, shuffling in the aisles, he only shook his head. Niania began to cry. In one of the side chapels she prayed to the Holy Mother. At another she prayed to St. Anthony. My brother and I prayed.

We left the church and walked around the square. Niania was crying, repeating over and over, "Mother of God, help me. Help me!" My brother and I didn't know what to do. All at once Niania grabbed us each by the hand. "*Matka Boska* will have heard our prayers," she whispered fervently, pulling, rushing us back inside the church. The sacristan was gone. We searched. We crawled under pews as before. It was useless.

Niania was not upset about an ordinary jacket. This was the jacket in which she had hidden the jewelry Mother had brought along with the linens the day we had left for Niania's village. Niania had sewn the jewelry into the seams of her jacket. "I hope I never have to use this," she had said. In the country we had gotten by bartering only the linen. I had never seen Niania cut the seams of her jacket to pull out any of the jewelry. Whoever had found and taken the jacket, even without knowing about the secret treasures hidden in the seams, probably thought herself lucky to have come upon a decent piece of clothing to wear or to exchange for something on the black market.

I didn't want Niania to get one of her headaches. "It must have been God's will," I tried to calm her.

"Yes, God's will," my brother echoed. "Don't cry anymore, Nianiusiu."

All during our crazy search I didn't say what I was thinking. The jacket had been Niania's. The treasure in its seams was Jewish. That may have been why the Holy Mother had ignored our prayers.

I don't know how Niania was able to keep in touch

with Mother in those days. Somehow she did. A few days after the jacket had been lost, all four of us met in a secluded area of the park.

It was a warm day, and the sun was shining. We sat on a bench. Mother told us how, after the raid on the ghetto, she had managed to escape over the same bridge that my brother and I had crossed. I thought of the two Nazi guards who had been smoking and laughing on the embankment under the bridge the day my brother and I had sneaked out in broad daylight. "A heavy storm started that evening," Mother said. "I am not even sure the bridge was guarded. I just walked out." The ghetto was empty now. Liquidated. Without false papers like Mother's, Uncle Samuel, Aunt Bella, and Raisa didn't dare walk out. They had been taken to a work camp in Płaszów outside Kraków. They were still alive.

"I have a job," Mother said. Her false papers continued to be convincing. Not only did she get a job, but it was in the kitchen of a Nazi family living in Kraków. I had no idea if Mother could cook. There was a cook in our household before the war. I had never eaten a meal prepared by Mother. She spoke German well. That in itself would make her suspect. In Poland it was often Jews who spoke German. "I don't know what will be." Mother sighed. "For now I have a roof over my head. And food."

Niania had been quietly fidgeting with the buttons on her dress. I knew she was waiting, frightened of the moment she would have to tell Mother about the lost jacket. Finally she just came out with it.

"Ach, *Boże mój,* how could you have been such an idiot!" Mother was wringing her hands and screaming at Niania. *"Boże mój,* what stupidity!"

"I am so sorry . . . so sorry," Niania whimpered. "I am so sorry." Mother went right on berating her.

"Sch, be quiet!" I tried to get them both to stop the whining and the shouting. "Be quiet." I looked behind me. Out of some bushes a large barking dog came racing in our direction. I expected Nazis to follow, looking for trouble. The dog ran right by us. Then a boy carrying a stick came rushing after the dog. In a second both the dog and the boy had disappeared around the bend of the path. We were alone again. But I felt surrounded by danger. I could feel it coming from the dusty clumps of bushes. From the path winding toward the distance. From the clouds in the sky. And here was Mother yelling and screaming about lost trinkets.

I wanted to remind her that she had already brought us trouble. Showing up like that, without warning, in Niania's village. The first time I had seen Mother use her jewelry as barter was when she bribed the peasant who threatened to inform on us. Sure, it was important to have valuable things to trade. It was equally important not to draw attention to oneself. For the moment Niania had found a good shelter for the three of us. We were safe at the convent with the Benedictine sisters. Until the Nazis went away. Until the war came to an end, I wanted everything to stay as it was right now.

"It wasn't Niania's fault," my brother said quietly. "It was God's will."

Mother quieted down. She hugged my brother. She took Niania's hand. "God protect us all." She sighed. I hoped she didn't expect the Jewish God to protect us. Passing for a Catholic Polish woman among the Nazis she was working for, I hoped she had a rosary and remembered to cross herself when she talked about God.

11

WE WERE SITTING UNDER THE CHAPEL STAIRS
with Krysia. She had found a deck of cards somewhere.
Now she was trying to teach us a game. She was getting
impatient: "This is stupid! You girls will never learn."
She grabbed the cards out of our hands and threw them
on the ground. Then she tossed the ones she was holding onto the pile. I thought she was unfair. Even if my
brother and I learned how to play her game perfectly,
we wouldn't get anywhere with it. Krysia knew very
well that several of the cards were missing from the set.
My brother picked up the scattered cards and tucked
them into a crevice in the brick wall.

"I know something we can do," Krysia burst out.
"There is a carousel not far from the castle. Let's go
there!"

"Mama doesn't want us to go around by ourselves," my brother said sheepishly.

"Come on," Krysia taunted. "You are not babies."

No, not babies, I thought. It's just that we are Jews. You don't know that, Krysiu. You don't know that Niania is not our real mama, either. You don't know that my sister is my brother. In a way, keeping a big secret from Krysia, who thought she was so smart and knew everything, made me feel strong and daring.

Niania was lying down. A little while ago we had brought her one of her headache powders. She had probably fallen asleep. Wouldn't miss us. We could sneak away for a little while. I was so tired of pretending to be normal. And invisible. In broad daylight we were always hiding. "We'll go," I decided. My brother looked uncertain.

"Oh, come on!" I grabbed his arm. "Krysia is right." We would go for one ride on the carousel. We wouldn't be gone long. By the time Niania woke we would be back.

I remembered, from before the war, the old carousel in the park. Niania had sometimes taken me there. She had lifted me up onto one of the horses or pigs. Perched astride the carousel sculpture, I was as tall as Niania. I wrapped my arms around the wooden animal's neck. Niania stood by my side holding on to me. I loved the rush of air and the up-and-down rocking motion, the smell of the paint and shellac and city dust in my nostrils.

With Krysia, my brother and I walked through the front gates and out of the convent courtyard. We found ourselves walking independently on the street that led toward the river. No one paid any attention to us. It was a warm late afternoon in spring. I was excited. We had been living in the convent for several months. Sometimes we met Mother in the park or on a side street for a few moments. Niania made sure that we went far enough away from the convent to do this. We did not want to arouse suspicion the way we had in the country. Except for her headaches, Niania was not as angry and unhappy as before. In the convent chapel we could go to mass together every day. Or we could go to St. Mary's on the main square.

At a street crossing ahead I saw a group of kids in uniforms with two matrons in matching uniforms. Marching in the same direction we were heading. They stepped in unison. They wore little kerchiefs neatly tied around their necks and kepis on their heads at jaunty angles. I didn't want to let Krysia know that I feared being anywhere near this group. These Polish kids who had joined the Nazis were permitted to go to school. They strutted, feeling special, and sometimes they attacked Polish children who had not joined the Nazis. I cast a quick look at Krysia and couldn't tell what her reaction to this marching troop ahead of us might be.

Before we could get to where the carousel stood on the embankment under the massive Wawel Castle, we would have to cross a small bridge. Ever since the day my brother and I had escaped from the ghetto, I didn't like crossing bridges. I certainly did not want to be on the bridge at the same time as those Polish kids who pretended to be German.

"Wait." I slowed my pace. "Stop for a moment." Krysia immediately got impatient. "I have to tie my shoelace," I mumbled.

We shouldn't be doing this, I thought. We had only walked a few steps away from the safety of the convent, and already we were in danger. I was the one who had decided to go along with Krysia's challenge. It was stupid of me. I had always been a little scared of Krysia. Not because she might think that my brother and I were babies. But because she was a Polish girl, an Aryan girl. If she suspected who we really were, she could inform on us as well as anyone. I bent down and fumbled with my shoelaces. When I thought that the group of uniformed Polish kids had walked a safe enough distance ahead of us, I straightened up. I quickly looked at my brother. He had understood. "All right," I said pointedly to Krysia. "We can go on."

When we got to the bridge, the menacing group was way ahead of us. By the time we heard strains of the carousel music they were far, far away. Then I couldn't see them. I couldn't tell where they had gone. They were not on the embankment where the carousel stood.

There were some other amusements. Four tumblers were doing acrobatic acts. Taking turns, standing on top of one another's shoulders, they jumped, turning somersaults in the air. At one point the man lowest down collapsed. The others fell to the ground. They must have been hurt, but they pretended not to be. All four got up smiling. One of them walked around among us with a hat in his hand. Some people dropped a coin in his hat, grumbling a little while they did it. We didn't have any money to give him. And as tumblers they hadn't been very good.

Once before the war my aunt, the one who was deported with Grandmother and Grandfather, took me to the circus. There were elephants and horses. I did not like the smells of the animals. I did like the short blue-and-gold dress of the lady who stood up on top of a horse and fearlessly rode around the arena. And there was a man throwing a lot of balls into the air so fast one could not count them. He never dropped a single one. I liked clapping my hands at the end of the performance. At home, hoping for applause, I tried

POLAND

to stand up on the saddle on my rocking horse. I fell off and scraped my elbow and got a big bump on my nose. I didn't cry, pretended that I hadn't hurt myself. Niania got angry with me anyway.

Now we walked by an old man selling fava beans. He rolled up pieces of brown paper into cone-shaped containers and scooped the beans out of a pot with his hands. He held the bags invitingly between his fingers. My brother and I both loved fava beans. Ashamed at having no money, we walked by with our heads down.

The carousel was in motion. We stood watching. It turned faster and faster until the shapes and colors blended and blurred. And they unfolded again into the distinct shapes of horses and swans as the ride slowed and came to a stop. We saw that only a few people had been riding. Now the carousel man shouted, "Fifty *groszy* to ride." A woman with two children paid, and all three got on. The children climbed on and off the various animals until they finally settled for just the right one to ride on. The carousel man waited awhile before he started the carousel again. When that ride ended, no new people got on. Again the owner let the carousel go around empty.

The organ music sounded so festive. The horses, with their front legs raised in the air, posed so gracefully in their sculpted frozen leaps. The fanciful benches, decorated with roses and leaves in beautiful bright colors, waited for those who did not want to climb astride a horse. I looked toward the top canopy of red and white fluttering streamers.

"Nobody is riding," my brother whispered to Krysia. "Let's just stand here for a while. He'll let us ride for free," Krysia shrugged her shoulders and walked away.

In the near distance beyond the turning carousel the Wawel Castle loomed. I turned back to look at my Kraków. In the soft layers of air the city looked so like a beautiful painting in the pink and gold of an almost evening sky. I could see the tower of the town square and a little to the side the spire of *kościół Mariacki.* From where we now were I could no longer see the bridge we had crossed. I did not see the group of Hitler Youth kids anywhere. They must have gone marching off in the opposite direction into a little forest. I wondered if Niania was asleep.

Please, sweet Mary and Jesus, make the man let us ride on his merry-go-round! Feeling guilty for praying for such a silly thing, I prayed anyway, hoping that our little outing would not be in vain. That the man, in his dirty shirt and leather vest and his nasty-looking boots, who kept his carousel spinning with music and without riders, would at last let us climb on and have a ride. All he did was repeat "Fifty *groszy* to ride." Each time he said it, my prayers for a ride turned into a twinkling mirage. I felt as if I were waiting at a station for a train that was never going to stop for us.

"Shouldn't we just leave?" my brother whispered to me.

And then we saw Krysia. She had started running around and around and around. Trying to outrun it, she was circling furiously in the opposite direction of the turning carousel.

Out of nowhere, out of the woods, the uniformed troop reappeared. The menacing band I had tried to avoid by pretending to tie my shoelaces was swarming, shouting, hopping onto the carousel. The man smiled and said nothing about payment. My brother and I cowered and receded into the shadows.

The ride came to an end. The organ music quieted down. The riders got off, fell into their two regimented lines, and marched away behind the matrons. I had lost track of Krysia.

Then I heard. I heard terrible gasps. A raspy, choking cough. My brother and I found Krysia slumped on a bench, coughing and coughing and heaving and spitting dark red saliva. We didn't know what to do.

"You shouldn't have run around so much," I was saying desperately. "You shouldn't have been running so fast." I sounded like Niania. I didn't want to sound like that. Like a parent. It was bad enough for Krysia. She didn't want to be seen this way. And I didn't really want to be seen with her. All that coughing would surely call attention to us. My brother and I sat down on the bench on each side of our friend. The violent rasping cough sounded as if Krysia's lungs were trying to fly out of her body. The coughing went on for so long. By the time it quieted down, I thought, her lungs must be in shreds like torn tissue paper.

It was getting quite dark. Not many people were left. No one had been waiting to get onto the carousel for some time. Then I saw the owner coming toward us. I was sure that he was going to chase us away. Or inform on us. "All right, you three urchins," the carousel man said, "get on." He started the music.

For an instant I hesitated. I didn't believe the man. I didn't trust him. We had waited for so long for our chance to take this ride. Then I leaped onto one of the horses. My brother quickly climbed on the horse right next to mine. We sat astride waiting for the magical ride to begin. Ahead of us we saw Krysia easing herself into a stationary seat on the carousel. It looked like a carriage pulled by swans. It was really just a bench. Nothing that moved up and down. Krysia's coughing had tired her so much. It was easier to sit. Just to sit. Tomorrow she would make up some story. Krysia had become the one who was different. Separate.

The moon was rising behind Wawel Castle. The carousel picked up speed. Around and around and around we went, wind blowing, teasing my hair, the motion dancing right into my breath, into the pit of my stomach. It was such a short ride. In no time the carousel began to slow, slow, slow down. It eased to a stop.

The carousel owner did not smile when we hopped off our horses and Krysia got up from her swan carriage. My brother and I curtsied and thanked the nasty man for our ride. Krysia said nothing. She just began to walk quietly away.

Careful not to bother her, we let her stay a few steps ahead of us all the way back to the convent. She was angry at us for having been there to see her during an attack. She was ashamed of being sick. I was hoping she wouldn't start coughing again before we got back. By the time we crossed the bridge it was dark.

In the convent courtyard Niania ran toward us crying. Screaming, "Where have you been?" Right in front of Krysia, good and hard, she slapped my behind. Then she slapped my brother's.

"Don't ever disappear like that again. Don't you know better? Don't you know how dangerous this is for you?" She gestured wildly toward the gate. "How many times have I told you that you are never to walk out of here without me?"

All around people were hanging out of windows. Some of the sisters came running out of the chapel where they had been at vespers. Niania stopped screaming, probably deciding that making such a spectacle of us was more dangerous than our having been away from under her watchful eye for a couple of hours. Niania had paid no attention to Krysia, who had walked into the building.

When we came into the room where we all slept, Krysia's mother sat on the bed in her corner sewing. She smiled and mumbled something. I don't think she knew that her daughter had been gone. Krysia lay down on her bed. She didn't cough. She didn't say anything. She covered herself with a blanket. We heard nothing more from her that evening.

In the morning my brother and I sat on our bed waiting for our friend to get up. Her mother sat by her side looking for something in her leather case. The sisters brought a doctor. They bowed their heads and prayed. I knew that tuberculosis was a disease of the lungs. That the disease stopped one from breathing. Old Sister Ignacja was there.

"Come." She motioned to Niania and my brother and me to come closer, to join them in prayer. Krysia's eyes were open, but I could tell that she wasn't seeing anything. All afternoon she lay there. So quiet. So still. Why didn't she make any sounds? She was such a bossy girl. Why was she lying there not saying anything smart to anyone?

Her mother didn't cry when she knew Krysia was dead. She was confused. "But her cheeks looked so healthy," she kept repeating. "So rosy."

The nuns came and closed Krysia's eyes. They prayed quietly. All that day and night Krysia's body lay on her bed across the aisle from me. All night her nose pointed to the ceiling. War was all around. Everywhere people were threatened, carted away, deported, killed. Everywhere. But I had never spent a night in a room with a dead person before. Krysia was such a tease. Maybe she was just pretending. I kept hoping that she would wake up in the morning.

In the chapel there was a requiem mass for Krysia. She lay in a small white coffin the sisters had brought. She was dressed in a white dress. "From the girl's first communion." Her mother smiled. "Isn't she pretty?" Krysia's cheeks were as white as her dress. Around her folded hands was wrapped a rosary of pearly beads just like the one Niania had given to me.

Krysia's mother stayed on in the shelter of the convent. "It's because of the snake," she kept saying out loud. "The snake came. Everything is dirty because of the snake." She went on washing her lace blouse. Every night when the lights went out I heard the sound of wringing cloth and water dripping. In the morning she talked about the snake again and repaired her blouse.

12

WE WERE KNEELING TOGETHER WITH THE NUNS in the little chapel where not so long ago Krysia's body had been laid out in a coffin. Over the mix of out voices, singing a hymn, we heard, *"Alles raus!"* ("Everyone out!") and then the heavy steps running up the stairs. *"Juden! Wo sind die Juden?"* ("Jews! Where are the Jews?") Rifles in their arms, the Nazis came crashing in. *"Schnell! Alles raus! Schnell!"* ("Fast! Everyone out! Fast!")

The mass had been interrupted just before the communion. The soldiers rushed up to my brother and me and Niania, guns pointing straight at us. *"Raus! Raus!"* Now they were behind us. I felt a rifle butt in my rib. The chapel stairs were not steep. There were only a few steps down. But I stumbled, almost fell.

My brother was right behind me. And Niania was crying. *"Nie, nie, nein! Moje dzieci! Sie sind . . . moje dzieci."* ("No, no, no! They are my children.") She was mixing the few German words she knew with Polish. The Nazis, ignoring Niania, were shouting at the nuns. *"Alle! Alle Juden hier."* ("All Jews over here.") Demanding they hand over all Jews. The nuns protested, were shoved aside. In no time everyone Jewish had been flushed out. They had caught up with us at last. It was Christmas Day.

They lined us up facing the wall. I looked at the dark red bricks in front of me and waited for the shots. When the shouting continued and the shots didn't come, I noticed my breath hanging in thin puffs in the air. I was shaking and shivering. My coat and hat and a scarf had been left behind in the chapel. So that was it. I wasn't scared. I was freezing. I wasn't scared. Not the way I had been scared that day we had hidden in the attic in the ghetto. Niania was here. In the convent, among holy sisters, the Nazis could shout, but the Holy Mother would protect us.

Except for Niania, everybody who was not a Jew had stayed in the chapel. She sobbed and pleaded with the Germans in Polish. Insisted that we were her daughters. One of the Nazis began to laugh. He pushed my brother into a corner. He made him lift up his skirt and pull down his underpants. For a moment my brother's little circumcised penis flashed into view. *"Und du, bist du auch ein Knab!"* ("Are you a boy, too?") The Nazi signaled for me to pull my pants down, too. With trembling fingers, terrified, ready to obey, I groped under my skirt. Then the Nazi changed his mind, pushed me away, and let it be.

I had never known that other Jewish people had been sheltered at the convent. There was a young man. A very pale, thin young woman I had never noticed before. A woman who walked with a limp. I had seen her on the soup line with her bowl and her cane. A woman and her teenaged son. I had seen them. Both of them had blond hair. I had never thought they were Jewish. The nuns had hidden us in broad daylight. We had all blended quietly into the life at the Benedictine shelter. A thought had time to cross my mind. I had never seen any of these people at mass. They were *Juden*. And I had become one of the *Juden*. Now all of us *verfluchte Juden* had been found out. Now we belonged to the Nazis.

With the rest of their catch, the Nazis shoved my brother and me toward a canvas-covered truck that they had parked in front of the entrance to the courtyard of the convent. The body of the truck sat high on the wheels. Climbing onto it wasn't easy. I held on tightly, heaved myself up, and lifted one leg, then the other. I was on. My freezing, shaking limbs tingled with the effort. I felt a crazy flash of satisfaction. I watched my brother struggle. I didn't want to help him. The Nazis had to think we were strong and capable. Then he was in. There were other people already in the truck. Both men and women. They must have been rounded up somewhere else. Shivering, silent, they stared with empty eyes at the newcomers.

Then we saw Niania running toward the truck with our coats and caps and scarves. I was afraid the Nazis were going to shoot her. But they allowed her to throw our clothes into the truck. Still pleading and crying, she was shoved aside with the butt of a rifle. Right behind Niania, I saw Krysia's mother. She was wearing her lace blouse with no coat over it. She was smiling and waving a handkerchief.

As if they were closing a curtain, the Nazis pulled a canvas covering over the back of the truck. The engine started. The truck began to move. I had no idea where they were taking us. Why hadn't they shot us? Maybe they needed us for something. Above the rumbling of the motor and the sound of the cobblestones under the wheels I heard a woman's voice repeating over and over again, *"Ich kann arbeiten. Ich kann arbeiten."* ("I can work. I can work.")

On our walks with Niania we had often passed by this building with its rows of regimented square windows. This edifice with the strange-sounding theatrical name was as much part of our city as Suki-ennice and the great Church of St. Mary on the main square. And the public park where Niania would take me when I was very little. Where I fed the birds with stale bits of bread that Niania brought along in a paper bag. Where I had picked the little flowers that grew so close to the ground. Unlike friendly, open parts of the city this foreboding mass of a building rose up square and dense and full of menacing secrets.

"Very bad people . . . who have done terrible things are locked up here," Niania told us. "Terrible sinners are kept at Montelupi."

The very foreignness of the word *Montelupi* added to the distance between our life and the unimagina-ble lives of the people who were hidden somewhere behind the windows that turned a blind gaze on the world outside. Perhaps fearing the curse of an unseen evil eye, Niania would cross herself and hurry us by.

I remembered a story from the very beginning of the war. Niania and all the grown-ups had talked about it. In a mountain village a postman had been murdered. The attacker had escaped with the mail-bag full of money. Police were looking for this man everywhere. A young woman accidentally discovered him hiding in a barn on her father's farm. She rec-ognized him from a newspaper picture. She tried to run away, but the murderer chased her over the fields. Her father found her slashed and bloody body by a haystack.

I had had a dream then. I was lying in bed when the killer came to our house. He looked at me and put a heavy leather bag full of money on the floor. Niania came in. In one hand she carried the little frying pan she used to fry bacon in. Her other arm was raised the way I had seen in pictures of saints in church with her palm facing forward, her forefinger pointed to the picture of the angel above my bed. I woke up. Soon after I had had that dream, the murderer was captured and brought to Montelupi.

It was to this dreaded place that the canvas-covered truck delivered its catch that Christmas Day. Commands were thrown at us. We were to get off the truck. There was the sound of hinges grating. *"Juden,"* one Nazi explained to the two guards. We hadn't murdered anybody. We were here because we were Jews. Heavy iron doors were opening wide to receive us.

I was stiff and frozen, but it was easier to jump down from the truck than it had been to get up on it. My brother hopped down right after me. I heard someone behind me help the woman with the cane and the limp. I hoped she would stop her *"Ich kann arbeiten"* refrain and keep quiet. What if her constant insistence that she could work made the Nazis angry? Who knew how they would take it out on the rest of us? I tried not to look at anybody. Not at the other Jews in the transport. Not at the Nazis. As if by keeping my eyes averted, I would become unseen.

We were pushed beyond the entrance gates into a passageway. It was warmer than in the truck. Warmer than being outside. We were very quiet. All of us Jews were quiet. Even the woman with the cane wasn't saying anything. She limped along, keeping pace with the rest of us. I hoped that the tapping of her cane would distract attention from me and my brother. I wanted to shrink away. To fold into a small invisible thing that had no detectable smell. No breath. No flesh. No sound. I heard the grating of hinges. The doors of Montelupi Prison closed behind us.

The Nazis handed us over to two Polish prison guards. We walked down a long, dim corridor, all smudges and blackness, smelling of disinfectant and piss. From beyond the bolted doors on each side of the corridor we were trudging through, I could hear scraps of sounds. Voices murmuring. Shuffling of caged footsteps. A knocking.

The Nazis with their guns had stayed behind somewhere at the entrance gates. I was still not frightened, no. No. I was not frightened. I was ashamed, ashamed that we had been caught.

Ashamed that a Nazi had demanded that I pull down my pants.

And I did not yet believe that this was happening. All through the ride I had carried with me the hope that Niania had followed the truck. That any second she would appear from somewhere. All we had to do was to turn a corner and the dank-smelling corridor of Montelupi would dissolve. Niania would come toward us, carrying flowers. We would find ourselves among candles and incense, walking in a church procession. There at the end of the aisle from the altar the statue of the Virgin in her blue dress, with her feet on the globe, would smile down on us. The Nazi soldiers would regret the mistake they had made. "Oh, yes, we are sorry." They would bow to Niania. "You may take your daughters home with you."

"Stop here," one of the guards said. He stuck a key in the lock of the nearest cell door. The other guard was opening the door of the cell next to us. Both doors swung open. "In there," the guard said. My brother and I went first. Behind us two men and the woman with the cane followed quietly. We heard the shutting door reverberate behind us. Bang. Then another bang echoing nearby. The transport of Jews from the Benedictine convent and other hiding places had been divided and locked up in two cells in the prison of Montelupi.

Through the small high window with the heavy

crossed steel bars I could see gray squares of sky. Two other people were crouched in the corner of the cell. The newly arrived group stood uncertainly in the middle.

"How long have they kept you here?" the woman with the cane asked. As if she were asking what time the next train was arriving. "I will convince them that I can work." She was a very ugly woman. She wore glasses and had a big nose. But just then she reminded me of Krysia's beautiful, demented mother repeating, "It was the snake. All because of the snake."

"Three weeks," a man sitting on a stool in the corner of the cell mumbled. "We will be let go on New Year's Day." He didn't sound crazy. Could it be possible that the Nazis were planning to hold us for a short time because that was what they were supposed to do? And then let us go? Even now they might be sending for Niania, to arrange with her to come for us.

There were two other wooden stools in the cell. The woman with the cane sat down on one. Her leg stretched stiffly in front of her. There were footsteps outside. Keys rattled. A key probed and turned. From that moment on every time I heard that key in the lock, I thought that this time someone was coming to tell us we were leaving. The door would open. And we would walk down the corridor. And out through the portal to the street. And to Niania.

The door of the cell opened. A tall man in a partial Nazi uniform came in. He was bare headed, blond. Very good looking. He didn't wear a jacket. His boots were elegantly shined. We had been in the cell for only a few minutes. I had not yet noticed the bucket in the corner with a wooden plank over it. How could I have missed the acrid, sour smell? That was where prisoners had been peeing and shitting. The soldier picked up the full pail and set down an empty one. Nobody said anything. He didn't carry a rifle. He carried an empty pail. An ordinary pail. The kind used to dip a rag in to clean a floor. Or for milking a cow. The thought of milk made me remember that we had had nothing to eat.

And then I panicked. That's why we are here, I thought. That's why we are here. They are going to starve us to death. I grabbed hold of the Nazi's boot. I knelt down. *"Milch, bitte, bitte,"* I whispered. *"Und etwas Brot."* ("Milk, please, please. And some bread.") I grabbed his hand and kissed it. He was startled. I looked up into furious blue eyes. The man didn't say anything. I knew he had intended to kick me away. Then he just shook me off as if I had been a yelping, not especially dangerous dog. I let go of his hand. He turned and walked out, taking with him the full stinking pail. I could see the pistol in a holster on his belt. The cell door slammed, and the key turned in the rusty lock.

My brother and I, settling into a corner of the now crowded cell, had spread our coats on the floor. "We have to be patient," I whispered to him. "Until Niania comes." Then I must have dozed off. I woke to the sound of keys turning again. My brother was rubbing his eyes. My first sleepy thought—Niania! Niania!—flew out to beyond the door.

We smelled food. The door opened. A guard wheeled in a bucket the size of a pickle barrel. He gave each of the new arrivals a banged-up tin bowl or cup. He ladled out a watery cabbage soup. From a sack slung over his shoulder each of us was handed a small piece of hard black bread. This guard didn't wear a uniform. He was unshaved. He looked like the peasants we had become used to fearing in the country. He was a man just working in the prison. Perhaps he was a prisoner himself.

"When will they let us go?" the woman with the cane asked in German. The guard didn't understand. She repeated the question in Polish. Several other people came out with whispered questions.

The man shrugged his shoulders. *"Ja nie wiem nic."* ("I know nothing.") Pushing the soup barrel on its wheeled clattering wooden plank in front of him, he turned his back on the inmates. Again we heard the screech of hinges. The heavy shutting of the cell door. The twisting of the key.

I looked at my brother. I could tell he didn't care what the soup tasted like. He was hungry. I was hungry. We set upon the watery slops. We had no spoons. We slurped the soup and gratefully chewed the stale bread.

I thought sadly of the Christmas that had been taken away from us. In the convent preparations for the special Christmas Day service had been going on for several weeks. Before the raid we had practiced Christmas songs. The sisters had liked our singing. Would they miss our voices? How many days till the New Year? I listened for sounds outside the cell. Surely any minute something would change. Yes, the cell door opened. But only when we smelled cabbage coming closer.

Even these moments we looked to with eager anticipation. The same Polish guard came in each time. Sometimes he came in with a pail of water and we washed our hands and faces. Once a day another guard would come in and take away the latrine bucket. I got used to using it in front of the others in the cell. I never could get used to the stench. I tasted it on my tongue. I felt it on my skin. The Nazi guard whose hand I had kissed never reappeared.

My brother and I didn't talk much. We tried to

rotate the clothes we were wearing. Taking what we wore closest to our skin, we carefully began going through the seams to get rid of the lice that hid there. Our fingers had become skillful at plowing through the stitched furrows. We would pop the lice one by one between our thumbnails. My scalp never stopped itching. The Nazis' war had permanently sprinkled us with lice.

Once late afternoon after the soup barrel had come and gone and the latrine bucket had been taken out, we heard footsteps that did not sound like those of the Polish guard with the food wagon.

The key turned. There they were. Two Nazis in full uniform. Rifles on their shoulders. *"Raus!"* They repeated their automatic refrain. *"Raus. Schnell!"*

We quickly threw on our coats. I tied my shoelaces and looked down to make sure my brother's were tied. Stepping out of the crowded cell into the prison corridor, I was overcome by a split second of crazy excitement. They had come to escort us out! Any minute now we would be on a Kraków street again. Niania would be there!

The cell next to ours had its door opened, too. I recognized several of the people from the convent transport. The pale, thin girl. The woman with the teenaged son. There was a large bundle of rags propped up against the wall. And then I saw that it was not a bundle of rags. It was a person. A large, shapeless woman. I couldn't tell if she was very fat or if she was just wearing so many layers of old clothes. She muttered something and smiled at my brother and me.

"It's Babcia," my brother whispered.

What? What was he babbling about? What? The paralyzed old grandmother from Łapanów? The dull fear that was beyond fear, which had wrapped me since the morning of the raid and had been lulled by the days in the prison cell, now spun off in a new direction. I kicked my brother, hoping he would not cry out. Hoping the others had not heard what he had said. I threw another look at the woman lying on the floor. Not at all sure that he wasn't right. "Don't be stupid," I whispered. "And keep quiet." He had to be wrong. He had to. Those people had been deported a long time ago. They were gone. They were dead. They were liquidated. Dead. I didn't want us to be connected to a Jewish relative. That would make everything worse for us when Niania came.

Along the same corridor that we had walked in—I could not be sure how many days ago, we walked toward the exit. Like a heavy sack, the old woman was pulled by the arm along the floor by one of the Nazis. She made no sound. Out on the street two more Nazis waited for us by the empty canvas-covered truck.

Just as when we had been brought here, we were made to scramble onto the truck. The Nazi guard who had been pulling the old woman along the ground grabbed her by both arms. Then the other Nazis grabbed her by the legs. Together they hoisted her onto the floor of the truck. Then they hopped on themselves. From one of the woman's wrists there trailed a length of bandage that had come undone. She lifted up her arm toward one of the guards. Like a skilled nurse, the German wound the dirty piece of fabric around her wrist and tucked in the loose corners. The woman smiled at him.

We were no longer behind the bolted doors of Montelupi Prison. Only the wheels and the rickety wooden planks of the truck and a canvas flap guarded by two Nazi guards separated us from the cobblestoned streets of Kraków. When the engine started, the Nazis bounced up and down on the floor of the truck just like the rest of us. Where were we going? Why had we not been shot already? Or was there still a chance that they would deliver my brother and me to Niania?

From a corner I heard again the voice of the woman with the cane: "*Ich kann arbeiten.*"

13

It was night when we drove through a gate and saw the guard towers and the barbed wire. I knew at once we had been delivered to a concentration camp. Inmates stood lined up in the quadrangle surrounded by barracks. They seemed to have been lined up just to greet the new transport. During one of our encounters Mother had said that the Kraków ghetto had been liquidated. The few people who remained had been taken to the camp in Płaszów. Now I thought I saw Raisa and Aunt Bella standing on a line with women prisoners. Was that where we were? In Płaszów? Searchlights blinded my eyes, and the sound of the Nazi voices shouting echoed between the barracks. We stood waiting. Contained and still. Our breathing poured smoke into the icy air. For five and a half years my brother and I had escaped. We had been running and hiding and pretending not to be Jews. We had been protected by Niania. During the years of flight I had heard the fearful word *Konzentrationslager* so many times. But I had never had a picture in my head of what a concentration camp might really be like. All I knew now was that what we had dreaded the most had finally happened. I was ten years old. My brother was eight. We were Jews. The Nazis had found us out and caught us at last.

The Nazis pushed and shoved and organized. I did not always understand what they were shouting. They began sorting. I held on to my brother's hand. The two younger men who had been with us on the transport from the convent were pushed aside. So was the pale young woman from the Benedictine convent. The woman who walked with the cane was pulled out. Then the woman who could not walk at all was dragged toward her and left lying next to her on the ground. The two men from our cell in Montelupi and the teenaged boy from the convent were also shoved into that group. His mother tried to follow him, but the guards pushed her back. The boy was quiet and didn't make any fuss.

Dragging the old woman along the snow, the guards marched this group back to the truck that had brought us. "They must be taking them to another barracks farther away," the boy's mother said. To herself. To us. To the air. Maybe they had left us behind because they had taken whom they needed. Maybe they would let us wait for Niania to come and get us. The truck drove away.

I don't know how much time passed before we heard the shots. I had no picture in my head of what was happening there, away from us, from where the sound of shooting had come. I did not know what I was supposed to be feeling or thinking. And then the woman whose boy had been taken from her began to scream. Horribly. Her screams sliced through the icy night, hung there, suspended, useless, beyond help. In the frozen stillness, the breathing of the camp inmates, the frozen puffs of air, must have stopped for a second.

The boy's mother threw herself on my brother, and began dragging him toward one of the guards. "Look at him!" she wailed. "Look at him! He is much younger! Why did you not take him?" She frightened us more than the Nazis did. The guards pulled the woman away from my brother and pushed him back toward me. He hadn't made a sound. I didn't dare to take his hand again. Why did they favor us over this woman? Maybe they liked us after all. Maybe Niania had talked to them. Maybe they would send for her. The cries of the woman whose son had been shot continued. The guards dragged her away. No more shots were heard.

We were ordered to the barracks. I saw Raisa coming toward me. Next thing I knew I was walking with her and Aunt Bella away from my brother. I was so afraid that that woman's screaming attack on my brother had singled him out. Since the raid on Christmas morning, when the Nazis demanded that we pull down our underpants, I had begun to think of my brother as a boy again. But we had been together in Montelupi. Now we had been separated. I was being pulled along with the women. I threw a quick look behind me. There was a group of men going in the opposite direction of the women's group I was with. My aunt and cousin were with me. I couldn't see my brother anymore.

We went inside one of the barracks. Away from the icy air, from the blinding glare of the searchlights, from the shoving and the shouting, from the woman who had tried too late to barter my brother for her son, from the burst of the rifle shots, I tried to speak. Where is my brother going? What will they do to my brother? I wanted to ask. Nothing came out. My tongue was stuck behind my teeth. I couldn't form words to ask the questions. It wasn't the cold anymore. It wasn't fear. I just couldn't speak. Somewhere behind my chattering teeth, my tongue was a dead fish, stuck, glued, useless.

Not far from the bunk that Raisa was sharing with her mother, she found one that was empty. The mattresses were burlap sacks filled with straw. They were better than the bare floor of the Montelupi Prison. In the bunk above mine two women were already lying down head to toe. "You get in there," Raisa whispered, pointing to the lower bunk. I did as I was told. There was a blanket that smelled of carbolic acid. I pulled it around myself and pressed against the wall. In this lower bunk I was left alone. All around I heard grunts and whispers from the women settling in for the night. Raisa slipped quietly away.

She came back clutching some things in the kind of string bag that people carried to the market. "Shh," she whispered. Out of a kerchief in the bag she unwrapped a half loaf of black bread. I had forgotten that I was hungry.

Raisa tore off a piece of the bread loaf and handed it to me. Then she brought out a hot-water bottle and a tin cup. When she poured out the liquid, I could smell tea. It was a miracle. Where did she manage to get all these good things? I forgot fear. I forgot Niania.

"What happened to my brother?" It finally came out of me. "Where is he?"

"Don't worry," she whispered. "He is with Uncle Samuel."

I took gulps of hot, fragrant liquid. I chewed and swallowed bread. And I fell away into darkness, into sleep, into black nothing.

Out of the darkness came the assault of a piercing, high-pitched alarm. I was confused only for a second before I remembered that I was waking up in a concentration camp. My first thought was that I had to go to the latrine. The night before I had noticed its smell somewhere to the right of the entrance to the barracks. All around me women were scrambling out of their bunks. Mumbling, adjusting their clothes, shuffling toward the exit. I hoped that I would be allowed to go pee very soon. "We have to line up outside." Raisa was at my side. "Every morning we are counted."

Above the gray-black oblong silhouettes of the barracks, their electric lights shrill against the winter sky, a thin sliver of a moon was fading, moving away from the night. Where was my brother?

The men lined up, facing us. That was when I saw Uncle Samuel. My brother stood right next to him. He saw me. We were shy strangers separated by an abyss of Nazis with rifles and dogs. They strutted back and forth between the lined-up male and female prisoners. In the freezing winter morning breath rose, forming clouds.

I straightened my shoulders and back, trying to look as big and strong as I could. I hoped my brother would think of doing the same. What if they had spared us the night before because they thought they could put us to work? What if we looked too small and weak? In the morning light it would be easier to see. Nothing stopped Nazis from shooting. Don't stand out! Don't be noticed! I prayed.

That woman. That boy's mother. Where was she this morning? I didn't dare take a real look around. Maybe they got tired of her screaming and just shot her, too. These morning thoughts were floating around in my head. Mostly colliding with the hope that I could hold on, that I would not pee in my pants.

I noticed the smell of food in the air. Over at the end of one of the barracks I saw two large vats from which steam was rising. Two prisoners were standing behind them with ladles ready. From somewhere within pockets in their clothing people were bringing out tin cups and bowls. I still had the tin cup that Raisa had left with me the night before. We were standing outside. But the smell and the tin bowls were just like in the prison. The women around us were beginning to form a line and move toward the food. My aunt and cousin didn't move. I looked at them wondering what I was supposed to do. Raisa was looking in the direction of her father.

Then something happened. Raisa yanked my hand. I was pulled along with her and her mother in the opposite direction of the food line toward a small building in the corner of the yard. We were hurrying toward a little stone house that might have stood at the end of a normal street in the world outside the camp. No one stopped us. We entered a door to a narrow hallway. We climbed up a short flight of stairs. We walked into a real room. There was a window with shutters and a wooden cupboard that stood against one wall. In a corner there was a small cot neatly made up with blankets. "Don't you need to make?" Aunt Bella said to me. She pointed to a door next to the main room. "It's in there."

I had not yet peed in my pants. With the relief I felt came a hint of hope. I had not been in a real toilet since we left our apartment at the beginning of the war. Even at the convent we never used the one that was there. There were too many people for just one toilet. Niania had kept a chamber pot for us under the bed. There was nothing nasty or embarrassing about our chamber pot. We had used one at home in our bedroom before the war.

I sat on the clean commode, prolonging the good feeling, and pulled the chain to flush. I listened to the sound of water cascading down and the tank above me refilling. I touched the holy medals around my neck.

When I came out of the toilet, my brother was standing in the room. Aunt Bella was taking off his coat. I still had mine on. I began to wiggle out of my coat and the itchy wool sweater I was wearing. For the first time since our arrival in this place, since our capture at Christmas, my body was entering the warmth of a room in a house. Then I saw the man sitting at the table. He was wearing a sweater and a cap on his short blond hair. His pants were tucked into his boots. He was very good looking. My feeling of comfort started to fade. We were being guarded by a Nazi in disguise. But no. He and Raisa were talking in Polish. Laughing.

That was when I saw the basket on the table. Out of it Raisa and Aunt Bella took out a loaf of dark bread and a slab of bacon. Its smoked odor tingled my nose and made saliva swish in my mouth. The man had a knife. He sliced bread for all of us and then sliced the bacon into thick slabs. Raisa put bacon on the bread and handed it around the table. There was also a *kiełbasa* that was cut up for us. And mustard. My brother's eyes were cast down. He had a smile on his face that made me think of a saying Niania often used: "*Śmieje się jak głupi do sera.*" ("He is laughing like a simpleton at a cheese.")

In the prison long dark days had slipped into dank nights of sleep. The interruptions by the guard bringing the barrel of watery cabbage soup or the removal of the latrine bucket had been welcome, even promising. All that had come to an end with the frightening events of the day and night before. And here we were sitting in a safe, warm room. We were being given good things to eat. We were being taken care of by people who smiled. I began to feel that something good was going to happen. It was going to happen soon. Perhaps I had not been wrong in thinking that we were special. My brother whispered, "Maybe she will come." Chewing delicious, velvety, smoky bacon, I nodded. Yes. Nianiusiu, I thought. You haven't come for us. But the Holy Mother has listened to you. She is with us.

After we had eaten and the rest of the food had been packed in the basket and put away in the cupboard, Aunt Bella lay down on the bed and fell asleep. My brother lay down next to her. Soon he, too, had fallen asleep.

Raisa continued to chat in whispers and laugh quietly with the handsome young man. Then he left the room and came back carrying a tin tub, the kind people used to scrub clothes on a washboard in. The tub was full of steaming water.

"You will have a real bath," Raisa said. She began to remove my layers of clothes. I refused to let her take my chain of medals away from me. "All right, all right." She rolled her eyes and let me be. When I had no clothes left on my body, my cousin helped me into the tin tub. I couldn't really sink in because the small tub would have overflowed. There I stood with the water reaching to just above my knees. Raisa's hands were all over me, soaping, rubbing my stomach, under my arms, between my legs. The man kept looking at me and smiling. I was ten years old. I did not like being naked in front of him. Why had Raisa not asked him to turn his back or leave the room?

In the safety of this room, away from concentration camp prisoners and guards, I ought to have loved the unexpected luxury of a bath in hot, soapy water. But I was being given a bath that seemed less to get me clean than for cousin Raisa to use me like a rubber doll and to laugh with a man who should not have been there to watch me.

The last time I had seen Raisa had been in the ghetto. Even then my beautiful cousin had no longer looked the way I had remembered her from before the war. She had chopped off her long, thick braids. Now her dark hair was a dull and dirty tangle that stuck out in uneven wisps. The graceful legs in white knee socks I had watched prancing down the street in a school parade were wrapped in wrinkled brown stockings. On her feet she wore a pair of old men's shoes. She had on two layers of skirts and a big brown sweater that had several holes in it. Did she have lice in her clothes and her hair the way I did?

Soon after my bath was finished, the man left. When darkness began to fall, we went down the stairs just in time for another lineup. No one questioned us. Again I was separated from my brother. He had slept most of the afternoon and still looked groggy. I watched him follow Uncle Samuel to the men's barracks.

14

A FEW DAYS LATER AT THE MORNING LINEUP I thought I caught a glimpse of the woman whose son had been shot. I hoped that she wouldn't look in my direction or my brother's. Things were going well. She would surely give us the evil eye. We had been selected to be special. To eat bread and smoked bacon with mustard and even hard-boiled eggs.

Some days, after Raisa had finished bathing me, she asked my brother to strip to the waist. She sponged him with the soapy water that I had just stepped out of. These rituals, the visits of the handsome young man, and the good food went on. Until one dark evening, just at the time of lights out, the siren sounded unexpectedly. We had to scramble out of our bunks and line up outside the barracks. Just as we had the night we arrived with our transport. From the commands in German I understood that the camp was to pack up. *Likwidacja.* (Liquidation.) That word was everywhere. The Nazis allowed the prisoners to scramble back to barracks, to their bunks to gather their possessions. Except for the rags on my body, my holy medals, my tin cup, and my rosary that Niania had given me, I had nothing.

Later that evening we walked through the camp gate. I thought of the people who had been with us when we had been brought in the canvas-covered truck. I thought of those who would never walk out. Their bodies forever left behind somewhere outside the barbed wire. We were leaving empty barracks. The searchlights had been turned off.

Kraków was not far away. I knew that. When we had been captured, the ride to Płaszów in the canvas truck had not been long. Now we walked through a dark woods. I walked with the women. The men were somewhere to the right or behind us. What was left of this camp was not a large group. Not far behind us the Nazi commandant was riding with his possessions on top of one of the two horse-drawn wagons. The guards trudged along the same as the rest of us. They were quieter than usual. This time we all seemed to be part of the same *likwidacja.*

Not long into the march I was nudged by Raisa at

my side. "You must step out now," my cousin whispered. I didn't understand. We were going through a sparse wooded area. I looked cautiously around me. The Nazis weren't shouting, but their guns were firmly set on their shoulders. Gloved hands poised on the leather straps. Ever ready to point and shoot.

"Step out, you must step out now," Aunt Bella was whispering. "Niania will be there, she is waiting for you. . . ." Niania had come as promised! For a moment I wanted to believe.

"Where is my brother?" I whispered. "I am not going without my brother."

"He will leave, too. He is with Uncle Samuel." My cousin shook my arm. "Step out now. We will, too. Step out." Three Nazis were marching just ahead of us. I was afraid to turn around to see how many were directly behind us.

I didn't believe Raisa. Why were they trying to fool me? "Why don't you step out first?" I whispered. "You and Aunt Bella go."

"We promised Niania to make sure you were safe first." How had they talked to Niania? Where? Why would Niania have communicated with Raisa and not with us? Now I was sure she was lying. This was a trick. There had to be a reason for it. They have arranged something with the Nazis, I thought. Raisa had become one of those Jews who were helping

Nazis. In exchange for some favor. Why hadn't we been shot the night we went to Płaszów? When they shot the old woman with the bandage on her wrist whom they dragged like a sack along the ground. And the woman with the limp and the cane. *"Ich kann arbeiten! Ich kann arbeiten!"* She had probably repeated those words until the bullets hit her. And that boy. Whose mother screamed, "Take him. Take him!" Trying to yank my brother out of the line. We were just as useless, and we had been spared. Now we were part of some kind of exchange. Now everyone had had enough of us. My aunt and my cousin wanted to be rid of us.

It was dark. But in January the trees were bare. The Nazis carried strong flashlights. It would be easy to spot anyone who tried to sneak away. This was not the same as that sleepy, warm afternoon when we had walked across a bridge out of the ghetto. I began to cry. That frightened the women around me. "Sch, sch, sch." We were creating a commotion. Any minute a guard could be upon us. Raisa stepped aside and stopped badgering me.

If I just kept walking straight ahead, didn't say anything, didn't look around, I would be safe. I didn't want to have anything to do with my aunt and cousin. Somewhere inside my raggedy clothes I could feel the chain of medals Niania had hung around my

121

neck. I stopped crying. I was surrounded by Jews. If I ignored them, I would be safe. My brother and I both would be safe.

I don't know how long we had been on the march when I found my brother. Now we walked together. Groups of men and women were not separated anymore. I think the Nazi guards were tired and almost couldn't be bothered. At one point the commandant allowed a few women to climb on the wagons and ride.

We were no longer in the woods. We marched on a snowy open road with fields all around. It was a dazzling night. The worn shoes my brother and I had on our feet were wrapped in rags and stuffed with pieces of paper. Somewhere under us, far below our bodies, crunching the snowy road, were our feet. We no longer felt them. Through the steely night we felt as if little motors were propelling us forward.

Above us the moon was full. The open sky was dense with stars. "How beautiful this is," I whispered to my brother. "Just think. If we were safe at home, we could never have known this."

"Niania would never have allowed us to be out like this," my brother said.

In the glow of the immense and cruel winter night we forgot hunger and thirst. On the feet that no longer belonged to us, lulled by the crunch of snow beneath them, we slept. Walking. Moving. Forward. In our frozen numbness we were nobody's children. We were free.

Sometime during the night several shots rang out. We heard screaming. We saw a woman kneeling in the field by the side of the road. A Nazi stood over her. In the bright moonlight a large stain was spreading. Coloring the snow red.

There were other shots. Then no more screams. Just volleys of the usual German shouting. We walked by. We walked on.

On a January night in 1945 we were walking to we didn't know where.

15

THAT FREEZING JANUARY night on the march out of Płaszów, in our drowsy, exhausted state, when we had lost all sense of time, of limbs, there was a new stir among the prisoners. Cutting through the breaths hanging in the icy air, we heard murmurs, whispers. . . . "Auschwitz . . . Auschwitz." Behind their veiling of barbed wire, silhouetted against a paling, still moon-lit sky, long rows of barracks loomed before us. Above us from the top of the entrance gate, wrought in iron, the almost hand-scripted letters proclaimed *"Arbeit Macht Frei."* ("Work makes one free.") Our shapeless mass of bodies shuffled forward. Stumbling along with my brother over frozen lumps of ice and snow, I trooped with the others through the gate. Intent on keeping the pace and not lagging behind, I had looked only down or ahead. When I finally cast a quick glance around, I saw how our transport had diminished.

Once my brother and I were together marching side by side, I had forgotten about Raisa and Aunt and Uncle. I hadn't really seen them since that moment at the beginning of the march when I refused to step out of the column. I didn't know what had happened to them. I didn't see around us any prisoners I might have recognized from Płaszów. Had they been shot in the woods? There had been that woman in the snowbank. Had there been other shootings? Maybe we had just slept on our feet for a really long time. Slept deeply enough not to hear shots.

And now we had come so far away from Kraków, from Niania. To this place that we had only heard talked about with dread and disbelief. Niania's talk of hell and sin had sometimes blended with the threats of Auschwitz. And this is where we had arrived.

A sick stench of burning cut through the icy air. It seemed to curl around the corners of the long barracks that stood in row upon row like huge, flat, inky smudges against the sky. It was then that I realized that the dreaded Auschwitz was empty.

Along the ground near the barracks water was pouring out of rusty pipes. I was thirsty, thirsty. . . . I leaned down quickly to catch some water in the tin cup that I had managed not to lose in the night. "You mustn't drink the water," my brother was pulling at my sleeve. "I heard a lady say that." I drank. I didn't care. I drank in gulps. . . . The taste of yellow sulfur on my tongue. Down my throat. I didn't care. I wanted to drink water. I needed to pee. I wanted to lie down somewhere.

The Nazis didn't bother sorting. They shoved groups of us into the empty barracks. My brother and I ended up in a lower bunk with not much hay left in the worn burlap casings. One of the Nazis pushed two women in with us and moved away. The women managed to find room in another bunk. These bunks, which were really no more than wooden shelves, were easier to settle into with two people than with four. I had had a bunk to myself in Płaszów. How I wished we could have stayed there. There we had been special. Lying next to my brother, on a shelf with some hay under us, wrapped in horrid smells, with rags on the skin of my own exhausted body, I didn't even care what they would do with us the next day . . . or the next. At this moment I wanted nothing, nothing. . . . Just not to be on the march, to be permitted to put my head down and not shuffle in snow . . . lying down, asleep . . . this was enough . . . it was good. . . .

Through a haze the camp alarm and the familiar shouts startled me out of a pleasant sleep under a feather bolster in a soft bed with clean sheets. It seemed only moments since I had fallen asleep. All around there were the shuffling, the grunts, and smells of waking prisoners.

"Where are we?" My brother was rubbing his eyes. His cap had fallen off. For a moment I couldn't answer him. I didn't know. Then I remembered the sign we had walked under. It seemed just minutes ago.

"Oświęcim," I whispered. "We are in Auschwitz."

There was something triumphant in knowing. It was the never knowing that made us into helpless lumps. For a tiny instant I sensed that my brother admired me. The way long ago I had admired Raisa. I found my brother's woolen cap tangled in the hay and burlap and handed it to him.

A Nazi came in and started to hurry us all out. Outside I saw that the moon had moved higher in the sky and was fading. The sky was turning rosy and gold. The morning was as beautiful as the previous night had been. The brutal, icy air blew away my drowsiness. At the end of the row of barracks I saw the chimney stacks. No smoke was curling out of them. *"Links!" "Links!"* The shouting started again. Always the shouting. *"Schnell! Links."* We had to turn left. *"Links."* Pushed toward the gate the same way we had arrived. Then I saw the train.

16

THERE WERE NO STEPS LEADING UP TO THE slatted cars of the train. My brother was shorter than I. One of the women reached down and helped him climb up through the opening. I had not seen any other children. Quickly I managed to hoist myself up, hoping that the Nazis hadn't paid enough attention to notice that there was no one among us as small as my brother and I. More and more people piled in. When the car was completely filled, when there was no room for another person, the Nazis pushed the door shut. I heard the iron crossbar sliding into place.

The boxcars on this train were all open at the top. The night sky had paled completely. There was a jolt. People bumped into one another. There was shuffling and grumbling. There was no possibility of finding a spot to sit down. My brother and I stood, tightly packed, in one corner of the boxcar. When someone moved, the smell got worse. The wheels under us began to turn. For a tiny fraction of a second a feeling of promise, like an electric shock, raced through my whole body. Then I remembered the day we had watched the loading of the Jewish transport from our hideaway in the abandoned building outside Kraków. Riding in a locked cattle train meant that we had become like those people we could barely see in the distance that day. What stupid promise did I imagine? The wheels on this train were not those of the train we had boarded to safety with Niania in the country. I looked at my brother. He was looking up at the sky.

The sun was high when the train began to slow down. Hinges, wheels under us, screeching, coming to a halt. I looked through the slats of the boxcar. I could see nothing but empty brown fields. The train came to a full stop. I heard the crunch of steps on the gravel near the tracks. The guards must have stepped out of the car they were riding in. I could hear the hissing and idling of the engine way up in the front of the train. The smoke drifted back above our heads. Why had we stopped? They will start unloading us, I thought. And pushing and shoving and sorting again. They will decide who is to be shot. I listened for the sounds of the slatted doors being pushed open. I reached for my brother's hand. The train was standing still. The doors stayed shut. For some reason that was a relief.

I had another problem. I needed a bucket. I didn't know if there was one in some part of the boxcar. If there was, I couldn't get through to it anyway. If I just crouched and relieved myself, who knew how long I would have to stand in my own mess. Trying to hold everything in, I had moved around as much as I was able in my spot. A little earlier I had reached under the layers of rags I had on and managed to pull aside the crotch of my underpants. I had spread my legs carefully and peed. Nobody had noticed. Or nobody cared. By the time the train had come to this stop, the pressure had become much worse. I was scared of going in my pants. I was ashamed. I had to do something. Using the slats of the cattle car as a ladder, I climbed to the top. With my back to the brown fields, I perched, holding on with one hand, with the other managing to pull my pants down to my knees. I was used to balancing over the big holes of outhouses with flies buzzing all around. I was as afraid of a Nazi shooting me in the behind as I was ashamed of shitting in my pants. I concentrated. I prayed. Below my naked buttocks I could hear the measured steps of the guards strutting up and down by the side of the train.

What if they saw me sitting up there and thought I was trying to escape? Then through my lower body there came a smooth rush of quick relief. I didn't wipe. Just as I started to climb back down, the train began to move. Safely back on the floor of the boxcar with my brother and the mass of bodies all around me, I felt triumph, almost joy.

Throughout the journey we continued to stand upright. When a prisoner, hoping to be able to sit down for a moment, tried to push someone aside, we heard arguing and fighting. My brother and I were small. We took up less space. We had managed to stay in a corner leaning against the side of the boxcar. To have been stuck in the middle would have been worse.

I must have slept. Standing up. When the train rumbled to another stop, it was morning again. We had been riding for a whole day and another night. This time the guards did pull aside the slatted wooden doors. With their usual shouting they began hurrying us off the train. We were facing a barbed-wire fence. Before us guards had already opened the gate. Beyond that, beyond the rows of barracks I saw a brick chimney with smoke curling in the thin January air.

We were moving toward the opened doors of our boxcar when we saw the body. Stiff as a wet rag that had been left outdoors in winter. The person must have fallen asleep and been trampled to death. I couldn't tell if it was a man or a woman. It was a body in rags. I never heard anything. We never knew. It hadn't happened in our packed corner of the boxcar.

It was a big jump from the opened cattle car to the ground. Whatever happened next, it was good to be out of that stinking boxcar. We followed the rest of the people through the camp gates. Holding hands, my brother and I tried to maneuver, staying hidden as much as possible. Walking stiffly, shuffling from one foot to the other, hoping that we would merge and disappear into the large mass of moving bodies. Not be noticed. Not be singled out. We were on our own in this camp. In my head I kept hearing, *Ich kann arbeiten*. How could the Nazis not notice how small, how useless we were? Again I heard the sound of a closing gate. I wanted to turn around to look. I didn't dare.

At the end of the lane of barracks, surrounded by several uniformed guards, stood a Nazi I thought looked more important than the others. He must have been the commandant. As we passed, he pointed with what looked like a riding crop. *"Rechts! Links!"* ("Right! Left!") The shouts echoed. For a split second I looked right, in the direction of the brick chimney and the smoke. I quickly pulled my brother along with the group going to the left. I don't know if we had been intended to go right, in the direction of the chimneys. All through the war I had heard rumors of gas chambers, of corpses burning. In a fraction of a second I decided that away from the chimneys was safer.

Somewhere on the march out of Płaszów that icy night, my brother and I had lost contact with Uncle Samuel and Aunt Bella and Raisa. They didn't matter to me anymore. First they had pretended to take care of us. And then they had lied. They had tried to trick us. The failures of the grown-ups around us had landed us in this place. And here we were, my brother and I, shuffling along in yet another line in yet another concentration camp. I didn't know at first what this one was called.

We were lined up in a barracks. We were told to take off our clothes. It was only then I saw that there were only women all around us. Had there been only women on the train? Wrapped in all those rags, I had stopped thinking of people as men and women. Only bodies in rags. Naked, we filed past uniformed matrons who sat behind tables. With little wooden spatulas these women efficiently scooped some kind of white paste out of buckets and smeared a gob on everyone's crotch. No one reacted to my brother.

Then one of the matrons came toward me holding

scissors and a razor. I knew what this was about. Most of the naked women around us had shaved heads. Some had covered them with caps or kerchiefs. I was pushed into a chair. "No, no, please." I clutched my hair desperately. *"Nein, nein, bitte,"* I pleaded feebly in German. The camp matron didn't look mean. She didn't hit me. She simply moved my hands away from my head, away from my hair. Two quick snips with the sharp shears and my braids fell to the ground. Then the razor clicked and scraped until not a hair was left on my head. My scalp wasn't cut. I wasn't hurt. I could have been a piece of wood the woman had been told to polish.

I didn't dare cry. I put my knit cap on. Several other women with hair still on their heads followed me into the chair to be shaved. My brother's hair was spared. Perhaps the woman with the razor decided that his hair didn't hide as many lice. My brother's hair was short, and it was blond. It had never been as thick as mine. Even though I was only one of many shaved heads surrounding me, I felt singled out for being especially *verflucht*. I had loved my long braids. Again I was horribly ashamed.

It was then I overheard a woman whisper to another that we were in a camp called Ravensbrück. We were ordered to go back to find our clothes. While we had stood in line, our piles of rags had been sprayed with some kind of powder. I thought it was poison and tried not to breathe. We put our clothes back on. They divided us into groups. My brother and I trooped along to one of the barracks. I breathed again. Nothing happened. I was still alive. My brother was with me.

In the barracks we found a bunk that was empty. Somehow we managed to stay on our storage shelf by ourselves. Earlier I heard some of the women from our transport talking in Polish about the dirty Romanians and Hungarians. Four women in thick layers of rags were sleeping in the bunk below the one that my brother and I were in. We were packed with bodies of hungry, dirty, quarrelsome women, mumbling and hissing at one another in languages we didn't understand. Płaszów had been a much smaller camp. And there we had been privileged and fed and taken care of.

All of us were used to being called dirty, filthy, *verfluchte*. As long as we believed the Romanians and Hungarians were the dirtiest, we could imagine that we were cleaner, we were better. Still, we were in a barracks surrounded by them. I whispered to my brother, "Even the way they talk sounds dirty."

We seemed to have been forgotten on the edges of the camp routines. After the morning lineups, we watched

groups of the women surrounded by guards marching off to somewhere. In the evenings they were
brought back. Exhausted and grumbling, they piled
into the crowded bunks around us. Except when we
lined up with our tin bowls at mealtimes, we cowered in corners, trying to stay invisible. We drank the
water that tasted of sulfur. The slops we received in
our tin cups were only just enough to pale the hunger. The cabbage leaf floating in the liquid teased
my taste buds with the memory of something delicious eaten long ago. Once I found a raw potato in
the mud. My brother and I took turns taking bites
out of it. Once we found a packet of salt and ate
that. In my deprived saliva there hovered memories
of butter and of bread, of fragrant, cooked potatoes,
the luminous remembrance of chunks of bacon or a
cup of hot chocolate.

Fear can be stifled by wave upon wave of hunger
that, not unlike nausea, never stopped gurgling in
my stomach. I didn't know that from hunger one
could cave into loss of consciousness, to hallucina-
tions. It never happened to me.

Somewhere, before Montelupi, before Płaszów,
my brother and I had been forced to leave ourselves.
Anchored in numbness, our bodies were nothing
but two hungry, itching lumps. Except for the lost
protection of Niania, I don't know if I mourned the

loss of anything. Feverish, always crouching, diarrhea dripping from my behind, I dreamed of a day
I could sleep in a soft bed with clean sheets and sit
on a toilet that flushed in a lavatory that had a door
that closed.

17

WE LAY ON OUR BUNK TERRIBLY WEAKENED, sick with colds and constant diarrhea. My brother was shivering and sweating. Next to him I kept dozing. In my dream I was about to take a bite out of crusty white bread with fresh butter. Before I had a chance to have a taste of the roll in my hand, it changed into a white-bellied fish that I knew was dead but still wiggled. I woke up choking and nauseated.

With our tin cups we took turns going for water from the pipe outside the barracks. I don't know how many times we hurried to the latrine. Except for those trips we stayed quietly in our corner. Mostly we slept.

We had to avoid being taken to the infirmary. Before we had even been captured, we used to hear of

experiments that were done by the doctors in camp hospitals. I didn't know what "experiments" meant. But I knew it was best always to look big and strong and healthy. We were sure it was best to keep illness secret from the Hungarians and Romanians. How could we be certain that they weren't informers?

"They are all around us," my brother said. "We can't hide from them."

"They won't notice," I said. "All they do is squabble with each other."

One night I dreamed that I was taking a hot bath in a great big tub. Feeling warm and relaxed, I woke up with streams of diarrhea running out of me and all over our bunk.

"I am sorry." I began to whimper. "I am sorry. I couldn't help. . . . I couldn't!"

"Don't cry," my brother whispered, moving away from me. "They will hear us. Be quiet."

I crept to the water pipe. I had been sleeping on my back. The gluey liquid had reached almost all the way up to the nape of my neck. For a fraction of a second a wild thought ran through my head: I am glad that I don't have long hanks of hair to clean. I tore off the lower layers of my clothes. Shaking and desperate not to be seen, I wetted and squeezed the stinking mess under the running water. The outer layers of my clothes had not been soaked through.

With the rinsed parts I sponged off my back and my thighs and put on what remained of my dry rags. I worked so fast I forgot how bitter cold it was. Before I crept back inside the barracks, I threw a quick look around. There was no one awake. I hadn't been seen. Everything was quiet.

I had not completely soiled my brother's part of the bunk. I mopped what there was of straw and burlap that served as a mattress. I forced my bundle of rinsed rags into a crevice between boards near our bunk. I hoped they would dry. If I had not quite been able to wash the stench out, it would just blend with the constant smells of the latrines and the diarrhea spills all over the campgrounds anyway. Everybody was sick from the cabbage slops and the water.

Trying not to touch my brother with any part of my body, I crept back into my corner of the bunk. I was thirsty and weak and ashamed. My brother was sick, too. But I was the one who had dirtied us both. If we were found out, they would surely finish us this time. And it would be all my fault.

Then, just about the time when I could no longer imagine life without diarrhea, we got better. Above the barracks, beyond the barbed wire, the light in the sky was changing. It wasn't as cold as before. Snow had not fallen for a while.

Two Polish women came one morning and said that my brother and I should follow them. We had not talked to anyone in our barracks. Even if we had wanted to, we couldn't understand anything the Hungarians and Romanians were saying. In the barracks we were now taken to, all the women spoke Polish. Each one seemed to occupy a separate bunk. One of them had hair left on her head. It was short, but it didn't look like hair that was growing after it had been shaved.

She was called *pani* Marina. She and another woman tucked us into a bunk with surprisingly clean blankets. For the first time since we had begun the march out of Płaszów, grown-up persons were taking care of us and treating us like children.

I began to notice the quiet but constant buzz of crackling sounds coming out of *pani* Marina's corner. On a wooden crate covered with a rag there was what I recognized to be a radio. Long cords connected it to a wire with earphones. *Pani* Marina put them on her head and listened intently. When she took the earphones off, another woman immediately took her place. Several of the women took turns at the radio. What were they listening for? Why were they not being stopped? Then I realized that we had not seen any Nazi guards for several days.

"What is going on?" Cowering in a dark corner of

our bunk, my brother made me angry asking me such a question. How did he think I would have an answer for him? I was as confused as he was. Just not to be surrounded by the dirty, squabbling Hungarians and Romanians was good enough. The nice Polish ladies didn't even seem to be afraid of the Germans. And we could talk to them. Deep under layers of fear, for the first time since we had been deported, I felt growing in me a tiny grain of hopeful anticipation. If I was wrong about imagining that something good was about to happen, I didn't want my brother to know.

"Don't even think that any of this means that Niania will be coming," I snapped at him.

One evening *pani* Marina stood up from her radio and put down her earphones. "They are coming!" she said. "It will be soon." The women began to embrace one another and cry. Marina came over to my brother and me and hugged us both. I had not been in anyone's embrace for a long time. It was odd to be held closely and lovingly. She didn't have a dirty camp smell. "You will be all right," she said. Under her clothes I could feel *pani* Marina's thin body tremble. "All of us will be. They are coming." Tears were running down her cheeks. I didn't know who was coming, what would happen, but I trusted Marina and the joy that could be felt all around us.

Into our barracks the next day, from I didn't know

where, some of the Polish women brought a whole load of large, heavy cardboard boxes. My brother and I were given one each. We tore our boxes open and found that they were filled with canned foods. Included with the cans, attached to the lids, were little keys. When I inserted the key onto a flap on top of the tin can and rolled it back, a promising tiny gush of air escaped. Everyone was opening cans, laughing, talking, and eating. I was stunned. This was not a dream. The smell of all the different foods was real. They teased my nose and tongue. There were beans and meat that came in a squarish tin shaped like a brick. There were flat little cans of sardines, packets of chocolate wrapped in shiny foil and colored papers. We had not tasted chocolate since the beginning of the war. There were round cans of thick milk like heavy cream. The pungent tastes and textures of all these magical things to eat blended and churned in my mouth. Unchewed chunks of meat, washed down with gulps of the thick milk, slid down my throat and dropped into my empty belly. I forgot hunger. I forgot Niania. I looked at my brother. Surrounded with empty tins, his eyes glazed, he was taking bites out of a chocolate bar and shoving sardines into his mouth. He was slurping milk.

"Why are they not taking all this away from us?" I said.

"If they give Jews milk," my brother whispered, "things must be getting better."

We kept scooping foods out of can after can until we were as sick from the real food as we had been from the cabbage slops.

One brilliant April morning soldiers who were not Nazis came and opened the gates of the camp. Some of the women rushed forward and started to kiss and hug the soldiers. They looked surprised and probably didn't much like it. Leaving the barracks with my brother, I thought of all those years of running from city to country, of hiding. I thought of the lineups, the marching, the transports in trucks, the boxcar, the shouts and commands in the dreaded language. We had been scurrying vermin, and now we were walking away in broad daylight right under their Nazi noses.

They were the prisoners now. Stripped of their guns, their helmets, not shouting, the Nazis stood humbled in a clump with bared heads. Silent. Maybe they were relieved that they didn't have to be responsible for us anymore. Maybe they were sorry that they had been too sloppy or too slow. That they had neglected to shove us in their ovens.

I did not look directly into the faces of the captured Nazi guards. Out of habit I only cast a furtive sidelong glance in their direction. I didn't hold my head high. Under our feet the ground was as muddy outside the barbed wire as it had been on the inside. Who our rescuers were I didn't know. But the passing through the gates of the camp was dazzling. I felt as if we were walking in a halo of light. Around my neck I could feel the holy medals almost burning my skin. Niania was not there, but she had been right. A miraculous present had been sent to us. The Virgin and the Christ Child had protected us.

Red Cross buses waited outside the camp gates. We rode all day on muddy, deserted roads. Our bus driver wore gray overalls. He had curly blond hair sticking out from under a knit cap with zigzag patterns. I didn't understand the strange language he spoke to the soldier sitting right behind him. I didn't know where we were going. They were taking as away from Nazis. That was enough to make them angels.

On our laps we clutched new cartons of food. Already we were refining our eating. We tried to slow down. To chew the food before swallowing. We ate beans with the meat. Took sips of the milk. The chocolates we ate last.

In the evening the buses drove into a thick forest. There was no real road. The ride was bumpy. Overhead we heard a roar of airplanes. It was then that the bombing began. Bursts of fire exploded out of the sky.

The driver put on the brakes. The caravan of three buses came to a complete halt. Lights were turned off. Like large animals that know how to flatten themselves and be silent in time of danger, our buses waited quietly under the trees. When the shelling stopped, our buses moved slowly ahead in the darkness. This happened several times during the night.

I wasn't afraid. I was excited. I waited for the next bomb to explode. Waited for its flash to light up the woods. When the bombardment was at its worst, the driver of our bus talked calmly to us. We didn't understand what he was saying, but I knew he was trying to tell us that everything would be all right. Listening to the steady cadence of his voice and seeing his strong hands on the wheel, I knew that no Nazi would come out of the woods to drag us back. That we were finished with that part of madness and fear.

Far away I saw a fire burning in the forest.

When the sky began to pale, the shelling from the air stopped. The buses rolled on. I heard the women wondering whether we were going to *Szwecja* or *Szwajcaria. Schweden oder Schweiz. Pani* Marina was on our bus, too. She knew. "No, not Switzerland," she said. "*Szwecja.* We are going to Sweden." Eating chocolate had made me think of my father. I remembered how long ago he used to say that when I was a big girl, I would go to school in Switzerland. I was a big girl now. I was not going to Switzerland. I was riding on a bus going to Sweden. Where was Tatuś?

By morning we had reached a coast. I was sad to leave our bus. Our driver was not coming with us. He smiled and waved good-bye. He was staying with his bus. "He has to drive back," I heard someone in our transport say. "Many more people are waiting for rescue." The sky was so blue and clear. No more bombers in the air. I wanted our driver to stay safe.

We came across on a ferry to Sweden. *Szwecja.* *Sverige.* There was a festive air on the dock when we disembarked. There were people who thought that our arrival was special. Photographers were taking pictures. I was ashamed to be still clothed in the same layers of rags that I had on when we walked through the concentration camp gate. It was only yesterday, but it seemed as if years had passed. I looked back. On the other side, there, behind us, we had left a world of hunger and mud and stench and corpses.

SWEDEN

My brother and I at the sanatorium. Midsummer
celebration on June 24, 1945, about two months
after our rescue.

18

WE WERE TAKEN TO AN OFFICIAL BUILDING. ALL these people in white coats and jackets and aprons were nurses and doctors. I waited for commands, for shouting. There was none. Everyone was calm and quiet. Everything looked so clean.

A nurse took us to a washroom. There were two sinks with warm running water. We stripped and cleaned ourselves. I didn't remember what a clean towel felt like. I leaned down, letting warm water out of the tap pour on the stubble that had begun to sprout on my head. I couldn't stop feeling ashamed of it. Wrapped in towels around our middles, we were taken into a darkened room. There was a large machine and pipes and cables and there was a strange chemical smell in the air.

The nurse came toward me and tried to steer me toward the machine in the middle of the room. I got frightened again. Clutching my towel, I wiggled out of her hold. The nurse was speaking so calmly, but not understanding any of the words she was saying scared me as much as if she were shouting commands. How could I know that we weren't being tricked and fooled? All the food and niceness could just be part of another Nazi experiment!

"Don't touch me!" I cried. "Don't touch me!"

I was clutching my towel around my waist with one hand and pushing the nurse away from me. She turned and walked out of the darkened room. I heard the click of the doorknob behind her. We had been locked in! I was trembling. I rushed toward the door, turned the knob. The door was not locked. I looked at my brother. During my entire outburst he had not budged. He had just stood quietly in the middle of the room. I think he was more scared of me than anything else that was happening.

In a few moments the nurse came back. *Pani* Marina was with her.

"These nice Swedish people are giving everyone a medical examination." She tried to calm me.

"That's what the Germans used to pretend to do," I cried. I was proud to let *pani* Marina know that I knew such things.

"This is different," *pani* Marina said, smiling. "The nurse only wants to take an X-ray picture of your lungs." I saw that *pani* Marina was wearing a loose, clean gray smock.

"I just had an X-ray taken," she went on. "There is nothing to be frightened of." She then spoke in German to the nurse, who must have understood because she nodded and smiled. I trusted *pani* Marina. I let the nurse lead me toward the machine.

"This machine is called a roentgen." *Pani* Marina stayed by my side. "A man named Röntgen invented it so that doctors could take pictures of the inside of the body." The nurse gently placed me against a cold, flat, square surface on the front of the machine. My chin rested on a scooped-out part on top. The room went black for a moment. There was a click and a buzz. My lungs had been photographed. Then it was my brother's turn.

The nurse gestured for me to sit in a chair by a white table that was full of thin, gleaming instruments that looked like scissors and knives. She took my hand and pricked my middle finger so quickly I didn't know what had happened. I saw my blood drip into a little vial. The nurse put a piece of white gauze on the tiny spot that continued to bleed slightly. Then more blood was pulled with a syringe from the vein in the crook of my arm. I winced. Again I wanted to run away from all these people. My brother was so obedient and didn't make a sound when his finger was pricked and the blood drawn from his vein. I didn't make any more fuss. We were given clean gray overalls, not unlike the ones the bus driver had worn. And warm sweaters with colorful striped patterns and knitted hats to go with the sweaters. I was glad to have a nice hat to cover my head.

After we had put on our new clothes, we were led by the nurse to a large room with long tables. I hardly recognized people who had been with us on the buses. Everyone was washed and clean and wearing fresh, clean overalls just like the ones my brother and I had been given. I still could not quite believe that we were not in some other kind of concentration camp again. The overalls were made of coarse gray cotton. On my freshly washed skin they felt like the softest of silks. *Pani* Marina came over and hugged me. "You see." She smiled. "There was nothing to be scared of." I was ashamed that I had made a fuss.

We were seated at a table with a young woman who had talked to me on the bus. I knew she had no toes. They may have frozen during a march. And then they had been amputated in one of those concentration camp experiments. Her feet didn't bend. When she walked, she looked like a strange bird. She wasn't wearing shoes. She had been given colorful knit socks to put on.

"The doctor examined my feet." She laughed. "He told me that soon I will be able to dance again." Suddenly she leaped out of her seat at the table and began to twirl around and around, trying to waltz on her toeless stumps.

All the newly rescued clean people were sitting at tables and using knives and forks and spoons to eat off china plates. I had no memory of the last time I had eaten food served on a plate. My brother and I sat down to heaping plates of something golden and fragrant. It was an egg dish with bits of cut-up potatoes and meat, a taste I didn't recognize, had never tasted before. There was butter and bread and dry rough crackers with slices of cheese.

How could any of this be real? Quiet people in big white aprons were moving between the tables with pitchers pouring clear water or rich milk into glasses. Milk! Where was Niania? Why couldn't I show her all this? All I could do was raise my hands to my neck and feel my medals and rosary. Thank you, thank you, Holy Mother of God. Please let Niania know what good things are happening to us!

19

M Y BROTHER AND I WERE SICK. OUR LUNGS
were sick. And what they were sick with was tuberculosis. I looked in the mirror to see if my cheeks were
as red as Krysia's had been before she died. Both my
brother and I looked pale. We were driven in a motor-
car to the country. To a white building with columns
and rows of windows that stood on a hill surrounded
by woods. It was a house for the sick. A sanatorium.
Everyone there had tuberculosis. That made it seem less
frightening. All the people who took care of us continued to be kind. Even though we didn't understand what
anyone was saying, the words in this strange language
always sounded soothing and calm. I had begun to
believe that the people who were taking care of us were
not going to kill or hurt us because we were Jewish.

I was taken to a room with rows of white beds. I took off my overalls and sweater and put on the yellow pajamas that were laid out on the clean, freshly made-up bed. I kept the knit hat on my head and climbed in. There were girls sitting up in all the other beds. All of them had hair on their heads. They didn't say anything at first. They just stared at me. Then they began to whisper to each other and giggle. I was comfortable. I had had plenty of food to eat. I was clean. And then once again I became suspicious. What had they done with my brother? I had understood that he was taken to another ward for sick boys. Where that was I didn't know. I remembered the boy who was shot that night in Płaszów. And his mother tearing at my brother, screaming at the Nazis, "Why didn't you take him? Look at him! He is so much smaller."

I twisted my rosary in my hand and began to pray wildly and noisily in Polish and Latin. All the little girls stopped giggling and whispering. They probably got frightened. They rang for a nurse. I tried what words I knew in German, crying, *"Bruder, wo ist mein Bruder?"* ("Brother, where is my brother?") over and over again.

The nurse understood and took me up the stairs to a ward one floor up. My brother came out of a room and stood by the door. He looked shy. He wore blue pajamas. He was a boy.

"I don't understand what they are saying," I said.

"Don't be scared," he said. "Everything is so nice, Hanka." He looked happy and calm and clean. Not sick at all. "They give so much milk and butter. Don't be scared." Maybe my brother liked being allowed to be a boy at last. Staying in a room with other little boys.

Once I was sure that my brother was all right and had not been taken far away, I could fit myself into the safety of this place.

Along with the rest of my strangeness, I had brought my sickness from war and concentration camp. The other little girls were just sick. They had become sick at home. I don't think that they felt that they were being punished. Most of them were blond, their hair kept long or short by choice. My dark hair had been shaved off me against my will. Now that the dangers seemed to have ended and stubble had started to sprout all over my head, I still felt suspect. Somewhere along the way I must have done something wrong. I wasn't a dirty Jew anymore. But among nice people in this pleasant limbo, without language I was an orphaned mute.

The nurses were called sisters even though they did not wear habits and wimples like the nuns. The Benedictines had been good sisters. They had worked hard and fluttered in the turned-up skirts and sleeves of their brown habits. Not able to stop the Nazi hunters' canvas-covered truck that had taken us away from Niania, they had scattered, like a helpless flock of partridges. The Swedish sanatorium sisters wore dresses striped in blue with pleated skirts and cuffed long sleeves. Their white aprons had wide bands that crisscrossed in the back and buttoned at the waist. There came such comfort from the laundered, starched smell of their clothes, from the sane, quiet way they went about their daily routines. I liked the plain-looking Sister Anna and the more ethereal Sister Svea. Both wore their hair in tight rolls under starched caps.

There were other ladies who were not sisters. They did not wear the little caps on their heads. They brought food on trays and came once a day with mops and buckets to swab the floors with diluted milk. I didn't understand that part of cleaning at first. The milk must have made the linoleum floors extra shiny. They all moved quietly on rubber-soled shoes like a chorus of angels' helpers without wings.

Every night Sister Anna or Sister Svea came to say *"God natt."* Blankets and pillows were adjusted. Every one of us got a hug before the lights in the ward were turned out for the night.

We were supposed to eat everything on our plates. The less hungry little girls, whose illness had forced them to go to this sanatorium, who longed for their homes and families, were more picky about what they liked or didn't like to eat. They soon discovered that the mute monkey with a stubble of hair in their midst was a fine garbage can. They passed me their plates. I finished what the others in my ward didn't eat. In six months I was a fat little girl.

Rich food, I understood, was a good cure for tuberculosis. Poor Krysia should have been here. We both would have been cured by the Swedish sisters and the Swedish food. And I would have had someone to talk to while we were getting better.

There was so much food. Strange crackly breads that I had never tasted before. And dark breads with a sweet taste that hovered on the tongue long after the morsel had been swallowed. And butter! I had not tasted its fat, slithering, luxurious sweetness for so long. Rich egg dishes and cheeses and fish smothered in cream sauces that the later well-fed me began to dislike. And cakes, cakes. Brown, fragrant cakes, pale, sugary cookies. When I finally read books, only in fairy tales did I find such magical feasts.

It was the names of the foods, which were served three times a day and at snacks at teatime, that were the first words in my new vocabulary. *Knäckebröd. Pytt i panna. Lutfisk. Skinka. Sockerkaka.* The words tasted as good dropping off my tongue as the foods did going into my mouth. Sandwiches layered with cheese or sausage slices or cucumbers were called *smörgåsar. (Smörgåsbord* is a tableful of sandwiches and goodies, a sought-out buffet, a culinary feast in the language of international cuisines.)

At first I had to spend a lot of time in bed, getting up only to go to the toilet and to wash in the bathroom down the corridor. I don't know how soon I came to take for granted the luxury of the flushing toilet, the sink to wash in, the fresh towels. I had no lice in my stubby hair anymore, no lice in the seams of my pajamas. The sheets on my bed were so white, so clean. There was a feather bolster and soft pillows. These were miraculous pleasures after the filthy bunks barely filled with hay and burlap. For years my body, my skin had not felt the wrappings of such comfort.

When I was allowed to go outside for short periods of time, I lay on a chaise longue on a veranda looking at blue skies and listening to the wind brushing the trees all around us. The nurses served bouillon and hot chocolate. We napped. We breathed the clear, pure air of the north. The world I had just come from had been drained of transparent colors and fresh winds. How could it be that a short time after living in filth and fear, trying to survive on slops in Nazi concentration camps, I was in a place where people had milk to spare to clean floors with? I lay wrapped in layers of coziness, well fed, well cared for. Still later, when I could go with other patients for walks in the woods or on the sloping green grounds, I saw that the sanatorium was completely isolated. I never went to whatever town or village may have been nearby. I missed nothing. If this was illness, I would have liked to go on being sick forever.

On Sundays there were catechism sessions taught by Sister Svea. We sat in our beds and listened to that Sunday's lesson. My medals were around my neck as always. No one tried to take them away from me. But I no longer prayed aloud in Polish. Swedish words were growing in familiarity, becoming my friends. I loved to listen to the stories of the New Testament. In our ward there was a little foot-pedaled organ that spanned four octaves. Sister Anna pumped the pedals. Learning to sing songs with words that were carried along by the music was easier than making coherent sentences. Singing along with the other girls was soon not difficult at all.

The Swedish people were Protestant. I soon discovered that Martin Luther was more important than the Holy Mother. What would Niania have thought about a Christianity that did not glorify the Holy Mother and all the saints? Where was Niania? Where was Mother? And Father? Where was he?

Six years had passed since the night he had left.

The only pretty things I had ever made with my hands had been the wreaths I made with the flowers that I picked in the country fields of Poland. There were teachers at the sanatorium who showed us how to use knitting needles and crochet hooks. Diligently following a pattern, I counted stitches and kept the yarn wrapped around my forefinger of my left hand. I loved the weight of the knitted material accumulating, growing, becoming more. I knitted doilies with a silky thread on a round needle. By carefully pulling out threads from squares of linen cloths, I learned to fringe edges or make hems with fine, small stitches. I loved the prick of the sewing needle obediently piercing the piece of cloth just exactly at the spot my hand guided it to. I learned how to embroider tea napkins with cross- or chain-stitched flower designs. And I loved watching the flowers growing on the cloth as much as I had loved the weight of berries filling a cup or a bouquet of field flowers getting heavier in my arms.

Sister Svea had given me a New Testament bound in white leather. The book had a yellow and a white ribbon attached at the top of the binding to be used as bookmarks. Before I was able to read Swedish, I liked turning the tissue-like pages. On the cover there was a glossy picture of Christ surrounded by children. I turned the little book in my hands. It felt so nice to the touch.

The sanatorium had a small lending library. There were books for children, illustrated stories about the adventures of a gentlemanly cat that spent his life being mocked by bully cats because as a kitten his tail had been bitten off by a big rat. To get the general sense of these childish stories was not difficult. I really loved them. But I was almost twelve years' old. I was forgetting the shame of my hair. It was growing. I didn't want to give the girls another reason to laugh at me.

I found a big book. Reading it, slowly turning page after page, the words in my new language were like so many sleeping beauties, captured behind layers of brambles and thorns. Gradually they began to come forward, detaching from their thorny underbrush. Shedding their moss. Slowly, at first, the words on the pages began to cooperate and perform. Sometimes teasingly. If I didn't understand one word, and there were many, the word next to it would send a clue, and I could guess and decipher what the meaning of a whole phrase might be. The mystery of the tale and the mystery of the language began to open up, allowing me to uncover their secrets. The first big book I read was a thick tome, a drama of religion and romance. I turned the pages and thrilled to the story of *The Robe*. "*Roman. Översatt från engelskan.*" ("Novel. Translated from the English.")

20

I HAD BEEN IN THE SANATORIUM FOR ABOUT a year. The war had been over for that long. One afternoon something happened that unexpectedly turned my life in a new direction. Sister Svea came into the ward followed by a man dressed in a black suit and wearing a hat. Under his arm he carried a bulging briefcase. He did not take off his black hat when he entered. He smiled, came toward my bed, and greeted me in Polish. I spoke Swedish well enough now to chatter with my roommates. Even with my brother I had begun to speak Swedish. With the entrance of this dark man, I felt the circle I had been able to stay inside of disintegrate. I felt threatened by something muddy and dark coming to reclaim me from the life I now lived in bright colors. With the sudden appearance of

165

this man I was instantly cordoned off from my new friends in the other beds. From the starched Swedish nurses. From the pleasant, sleepy, bolstered, well-fed life I had been miraculously flung into.

I wanted nothing beyond this sanatorium. I knew I was ill, but I never felt sick. I had never felt better. How could any of this be dangerous or even be called illness? Once a week there was a drawing of blood from the vein in my arm, and once a month a chest X-ray. It was a routine. There was no medicine to take. I wasn't scared. Since I had come to the sanatorium, no one had died lying in a bed next to mine with nose and feet pointing to the ceiling. The sisters gave me lengths of satin ribbons in various colors to tie around my head. My hair was growing.

"I brought you some little books that you ought to have," the dark man explained confidentially in Polish. "Jewish stories." On my bed he laid illustrated pamphlets. Not unlike those we used in the weekly catechism sessions with Sister Svea on Sundays.

I looked into the smiling face. A Jewish face with droopy eyelids and a big nose, tempting me with Jewish gifts. I was angry, angry!

"Get out of here," I began to scream in Polish. "I don't want these things! Get out of here!"

The man was startled. Sister Svea tried to calm me. "These are Jewish stories for you."

"I don't need Jewish stories," I cried in Swedish. "I am Christian." I threw the offerings laid out on my bolster on the floor. "Get these things out of here!"

Confused, the man bent down. He quickly gathered booklets and pictures and put them back into his briefcase. He was saying something to me. I knew he was trying to be nice. I didn't listen. I didn't trust him. I screamed, "Get out! Get out!" over and over again. Sister Svea, whispering, took the man's arm and led him out.

My roommates looked at me the way they had the first day I had been brought to the ward. I hid my face in the pillow and cried. I was so ashamed. I remembered Niania's mistrust of the Hasid on our balcony. How did that Jewish man find me here? How did he dare to visit? I lived in pristine surroundings with kind, quiet people who spoke a beautiful language that was becoming mine. I had come far away from those years of darkness and fear. I didn't want to be reeled back.

When I calmed down and lifted my face from my pillow, I noticed a piece of paper with something written on it lying on my night table. That man left it, I thought angrily; he won't let go of me! I wanted to tear up the piece of paper and throw it away. But before I did, I read what was written on the paper in Swedish. "Ask the nurse to write to these people.

They will try to look for family members in Poland."
There was the name of an association and an address
in Stockholm. The names of the agency people were
Swedish.

I didn't remember ever writing a letter to anyone. I
wasn't going to ask Sister Svea or anybody for help. I
would write to these people myself. I got some letter
paper from one of the other girls. They were always
writing letters home. I wrote my letter in Swedish.
Carefully checking my spelling, I explained how my
brother and I had been rescued and where we were at
the moment. And I wrote of the last time we had seen
Niania at the raid on the Benedictine convent. I gave
the address of the convent in Kraków. The next time
I saw Sister Anna I asked her to mail my letter. She
looked at me with surprise, but she took my letter.
She promised to put a stamp on it and to mail it.

Not long after that an astonished Sister Svea handed
me a letter with a Polish stamp on the envelope. I recognized my mother's handwriting. "Dearest, dearest
ones! We could not believe it. We could not believe.
Niania and I danced in the street crying and singing, 'The children are alive . . . the children are alive.'
Thank God, thank God!" was written on the piece
of thin letter paper with my mother's careful handwriting. A second sheet was from Niania. "I kiss you

both. I kiss your sweet eyebrows. I kiss your little feet. *Matka Boska* be forever thanked, forever praised." Niania wrote how she had had no trouble pulling my mother along to mass. They went to *kościoł Mariacki*. They had lit candles together. The joyful words went on and on. The two sheets of paper were carefully folded, but some words had smudged as if tears had fallen on the writing before the letter was mailed.

I ran to Sister Svea, waving my pieces of paper. "A letter from my *niania* and from Mother," I cried. "Please, bring my brother!" Other sisters and sanatorium help gathered. I know they thought that this time their refugee girl had finally gone mad. The girls in my room, even those who were not yet allowed out of bed, had come out to the corridor. My brother was brought from his room. We sat on chairs in Sister Svea's office, and both read the letters over and over again. Then, between crying and embarrassment, we translated the Polish words into Swedish.

I don't think that anyone really believed any of this until a few days later a letter from the agency in Stockholm arrived stating officially that the mother and the nanny of the girl and boy currently recuperating in the care of the sanatorium had been found.

Nothing changed in our daily life. We were the same children, the same patients following the same daily routines as before. But now we were no longer orphans. My brother and I wrote letters. Letters from Kraków came back. Niania and Mother were now sharing a small apartment they had found. Mother had some kind of job in an office. In one letter there came a photograph of Mother and Niania. They were walking down a wintry street in shoes with wooden soles. There were no shoes with leather soles available after the war, Mother explained in the letter.

I accepted all this, not really knowing how to put myself into something beyond my present life in the sanatorium. I spoke Swedish. I read books. I sang songs. I saw movies in the big social hall on the ground floor. One day a man came and gave a lecture on collecting stamps. It was probably boring, but I loved the way he talked and told stories about the different stamps that were neatly placed in transparent folders. Another time the sanatorium staff organized a talent show. One nurse played a waltz on the piano while another danced a ballet. She leaned forward, balancing on the toes of one leg, arms stretched out in front, her other leg extended behind her. That was called an arabesque. I had been asked to sing a song I had learned. I became so panicky when I looked at the people sitting on chairs in the audience I couldn't do it. I just stepped off the podium, curtsied and apologized, and ran out of the hall.

I had made friends. Brita, who had the bed next to mine, was a special friend. We had whispered conversations at night when the lights were turned out. "I want to become a nurse," Brita said. When she recovered, her father and older brother came to take her home one Sunday morning. A new girl who was really sick was put in Brita's bed. I missed my friend, but I wanted nothing to change. I didn't feel sick, so I didn't think that it was necessary to get better and recover. And I didn't want to leave. It never crossed my mind that my brother and I would ever have to leave if we didn't want to. I was happy.

Then something else happened. A letter came from Father. He had come back to Kraków. All during the war he had been in Russia. He had been captured by the Russians when he left Kraków that night a long time ago to flee the Nazis. First he was in a Russian camp. Then he had been let go. He had lived in Samarkand. He had run a little stand at a local market, selling trinkets, toys, caps, jewelry, cigarettes. The war was over now. Father, along with many former Polish prisoners, had been permitted or maybe forced to go home. I never knew which.

"Droga, kochana, córeczko!" ("Dear, darling, little daughter!") began his first letter to me. It was full of flowery words, as if after seven years of not having children he was trying out being a father in the words

on a page. Of course he had no way of knowing what had happened to my brother and me during all those long years of the war. Tatuś. He was just a word to me. An old word. A memory. In the next letter he included a photograph of himself, the kind of square little picture that gets stamped with a seal on identity papers. In the picture he looked exactly like my father.

Affectionate, joyous letters came from the trio in Kraków, constantly. Everything was promising and interesting. But none of this made me anticipate that I would have to give up my life at the sanatorium.

21

HERR (MR.) NILLSON, CARRYING MY SMALL
suitcase, and I stepped off the train. At three o'clock
in the afternoon it was dark. But it was a reasonable
darkness because it was the dark time of the year.
Outside the train station clanking tramways and a
few automobiles whizzed by. The street was clogged
with bundled-up bicycle riders.

My nose tingled in the icy air and delighted in the
gutsy, rough smell of gasoline and the odors from res-
taurants. Walking with this nice man along the well-lit
street where I had never been, I was once again surrounded by the brusque sounds of a city. I came to
think of how ever since I was very small I had loved
being a city girl. Among the many things the Nazis
had robbed me of was living in a city.

There, mounted high on the top of a Stockholm building, was a Suchard sign. Just like the one in Kraków. Blinking on and off in this city that I was seeing for the first time. Stockholm, Sweden. Suchard. For seven years I had not walked on a street that breathed with everyday life and sparkled with neon advertising signs. The memory of smells and sounds that had been wrenched from me was rushing back. I thought of the days before the war when my father had held my hand and we had walked on the streets of Kraków. "Look there, Hanusiu!" We had often looked up to where the Suchard chocolate sign flashed on top of a tall building. My father had been the owner of a small local chocolate factory. But Swiss chocolates were the finest. "I want the chocolates I sell to be as good as Suchard's," my father had said.

"You will go to a fine school in Switzerland." That, too, my father had often said. Naturally my father would have wanted me to go to school in such a fine place. In a place that made the best chocolates.

Herr Nillson had taken my arm and tucked it under his. My right side felt the warmth and support of his body. The sparkle of Stockholm wrapped itself around us. I was walking with a strange man, a nice man who wore polished shoes and who smelled good. I was not a four-year-old little girl anymore. On a lively street in this city where I had never been,

I was another person. I had evaded death from German soldiers. I had healed in a hospital. I was not sick anymore. I had survived. And almost, almost, for a little while, I felt like a girl simply walking home with her father.

"You speak Swedish like a native *skånska*." *Herr* Nillson had laughed when he met me. He thought it was odd to hear this dark-haired foreign girl speaking with the rustic, rounded inflections of speech common to the rural southern parts of Sweden. For almost two years I had never left the immediate area of the sanatorium. *Herr* Nillson was the first person from outside with whom I had spoken my newly acquired language.

It had been explained to me that I had recovered from my illness. I couldn't stay at a house for sick people anymore. When *Herr* Nillson came to gather me up at the sanatorium, I had to accept that I was going with him alone. My brother was still sick. Lucky, I thought, to be allowed to stay for a little while longer at the sanatorium.

Herr Nillson was taking me to a shelter for Polish refugee kids. "You will like being with people from your own country again," he said. He must have sensed instantly that he had not reassured me. "It is a fine place," he said quietly. "You will see. And it is only temporary," he added. "Don't be frightened."

The trip to Stockholm had taken several hours. My recovery to good health was sending me into unwanted exile, but the journey did not feel like a deportation or a flight. I loved sitting on a train with upholstered seats and watching the winter landscape rush by through the pristinely polished window. In the January cold of Sweden there had been no possibility of sticking my head out an open window and letting the wind whip my face and hair. The hair that had grown to shoulder length and was at last braided into two thick, stubby braids. They were still too short. But there was no more concentration camp stubble to be ashamed of.

We came to a quiet street away from the tramways and neon lights. After a ride to the third floor in a small cage elevator, we stood in front of a door with a brass plaque with "A. Nillson" engraved on it. *Herr* Nillson rang the bell. The door was opened by a gaunt lady, in a prim white apron over a brown dress. Except that her gray hair was tightly wound into a bun and her head was not covered in a wimple, she made me think of a Benedictine nun. She curtsied to *Herr* Nillson. I curtsied to her. She took my little suitcase and my coat and scarf.

"If Miss Stina would be so kind," *Herr* Nillson said, "our young traveler will have some tea and sandwiches."

My father and his family in Łapanów. My father is at the far right. This photograph was probably taken about the time of his bar mitzvah. (All the photographs from before 1945 survived either because my mother hid them in the seams of her clothing or my father carried them with him to Russia.)

My father's parents in Łapanów. The woman is Babcia. I never knew my father's father; he died just after I was born.

The Łapanów family again on the steps of their beer hall. Probably 1938–1939.

The back of the apartment building where my mother's parents and sister lived. Kraków, early 1930s.

Father at a cafe with a friend. Probably Vienna, 1933.

Mother in Kraków about the time I was born.

My mother's sister, who often read to me. Early 1930s.

Father skiing with a friend in Zakopane.
Probably 1938.

Swimming before the war. My father is at the center of
the photograph, sitting on a rock. To his right, Aunt
Bella, Uncle Samuel, and Cousin Raisa. I don't know the
others. Summer, 1938.

The picture of the angel that hung above my bed in Kraków. I had carried an image of this picture in my mind for years. A Catholic girl I met in New York recognized the picture from my description. She had a copy of it and lent it to me. I had the picture photographed and framed.

å små polskor har just anlänt me

My brother (RIGHT) and me (LEFT) just after we have disembarked from the ferry that carried us across the Baltic Sea to Sweden in the care of the Swedish Red Cross. This photograph was originally printed in a Swedish newspaper in May, 1945.

Mother is sitting and Niania is asleep by a haystack, somewhere outside of Kraków, right after the war.

Mother and Niania in Kraków after the liberation in 1945. This is the picture that they sent in an early letter to the sanatorium.

With my ward mates in the sanatorium in Sweden. I am standing in the center of the back row. The girl turning her head at the far left of the first row is my special friend, Brita. 1946.

My father in a photograph taken while he was still in Russia. 1946.

Mother in a photograph taken for her passport to Sweden. 1947.

In my new middy dress, new socks, and sandals, with my parents and a boarder from the *pensionat*. We are posing in front of the Parliament building in Stockholm. 1947.

More pictures from a summer Sunday in Stockholm. 1947.

Me, with constant ribbons in my hair.

On a park bench with my father.

With Mother and Father.

Mother, Father, the same friend from the *pensionat,* and me on a promenade by the water's edge during one of our Sunday walks in the summer of 1947. The Stockholm City Hall towers in the distance.

At the youth camp. Here we are wearing our Polish Scout uniforms. I am third from left. Spring, 1947.

Some of the lodgers in *fröken* Löwengård's *pensionat*. Mother is third from left. 1947.

...1 an outing with my classmates at the end of my first real school year. I am in the :ond row, second from the left. My teacher stands at the far right, just behind the :ond row of girls. Stockholm, 1948.

A local studio photograph with my brother, about the time of his bar mitzvah. Stockholm, 1949.

In the garden of the house where we lived in the spring after Niania's death. I had made my blouse and skirt in sewing class. A suburb of Stockholm, 1950.

Preparing to emigrate as a business student *(affärselev)*. This picture was taken for my passport issued by the Polish consulate in Stockholm. 1951.

I was twelve years old that late January afternoon when I was ushered into A. Nillson's elegant apartment in Stockholm, Sweden. For seven years, in or out of danger, I had lived and slept in hovels or public rooms with many other people. The convent. The concentration camp barracks. The sanatorium. Institutions. Since we had fled with Niania away from Kraków, I had not been in a private place where people had properly arranged tables and chairs and rugs and lamps. And servants.

"You may sit down." *Herr* Nillson smiled. In the beautiful sitting room I eased myself cautiously onto the edge of a wooden chair that stood by the door. There were pots with plants by the windows. There were lace curtains. Several paintings on twisted silk cords hung from moldings. There was a rug on the floor that made me think of the old kilim in my parents' apartment in Kraków. One whole wall was covered with books. I heard the sounds of piano music from somewhere in the building.

"No, sit here," *Herr* Nillson said, pointing to an elegant chair covered in a silky blue striped fabric.

I wished I had been a doll or a puppet. I wished someone would come and bend my arms and legs into the right angles so that I knew how to fit myself properly into the seat of the beautiful chair I had been asked to occupy. I had seen a movie one afternoon in the big hall in the sanatorium. It took place in France. The people moved and posed gracefully in splendid rooms. Ladies in gowns of silk sat on silk sofas and took little sips of tea out of pretty porcelain cups and delicate bites of little cakes. Gentlemen bowed and kissed the hands of the ladies.

I knew my body was clean. There were no lice in my newly grown hair. Or in the seams of the skirt and blouse and sweater that had come out of a freshly donated bundle. When I carefully eased myself down onto the seat, I could feel my wool stockings pull around my thighs as the home-sewn garters with the buttons dug into my buttocks. I sat on *Herr* Nillson's silk chair, still fearing that shameful dirt would seep through. In my head there were echoes of the Nazis' shouts: "*Schmutzige. Verfluchte, schmutzige Juden.*"

Herr Nillson sank easily into a large upholstered chair with curved arms.

Stina brought buttered bread and ham and tea on a tray. And cups and linen napkins. I took little bites of my sandwich and held my teacup as delicately as I could. I wanted to stay there with *Herr* Nillson forever.

Behind him I saw a half-opened door to a small room with a bed. *Herr* Nillson followed my gaze. "For tonight that is your room," he said. "Early tomorrow we will continue our journey." We both sipped from our teacups.

Herr Nillson told me about the work he did with refugees who had come to Sweden after the war. And about the interesting times I could expect at the Polish shelter and beyond. When it was time to go to bed, *Herr* Nillson took down a book from his crowded bookshelf. "This is for you," he said. "You may keep this."

Safely tucked in my suitcase were some catechism magazines that had been given out during Sunday school lessons at the sanatorium. And my miniature copy of the New Testament with pages thin and delicate and filled with beautiful pictures of the Holy Family, the gift from Sister Svea. Now I would add another book to my belongings. I thanked *Herr* Nillson for the volume of Selma Lagerlöf stories. I thanked the stern-looking Stina for the food. Everyone said, *"God natt."*

I went into my private room and closed the door. Tomorrow I was going to a place that would have no barbed wire around it. There would be no Nazis with guns. There would be no shooting. But again I would be living in an institution. Under the large soft bolster with my head on a pillow edged with lace, I fell asleep reading a tale by Selma Lagerlöf.

In the morning Stina brought hot water in a pitcher to my room. She looked at me soberly and directly but never smiled when I said, *"Tack så mycket."* ("Thank you very much.") She poured the water into the washbowl and mumbled something as she left the room. I washed my hands and face. With the washcloth I sponged carefully around my neck, under my arms, and between my legs. I had learned how to do that in the sanatorium. With the larger towels they had always given us small cloths. *Stjärtlappar,* they were called. Little cloths to sponge your ass with. Along with Selma Lagerlöf, the pajamas I had slept in went back into my suitcase. I dressed quickly in the clothes I had worn the day before.

It was still dark outside when we left the building. Cold and crisp. Again the street was full of bicyclists. *Herr* Nillson had taken my suitcase. He had already told me that the bus station was not very far. How I wished it were! How I wished the bus station and all the buses had disappeared to another side of the world.

"A very good place. You will see." *Herr* Nillson again put my arm under his. "Not very far from Stockholm."

I heard words. Only words. At the station we found the bus to Kummelnäs. I inhaled the smell of the exhaust fumes filling the air. On a cold gray day in January I was once again being taken away from a city with buildings and neon signs and tramways.

Very few people were boarding our bus. I took my seat next to *Herr* Nillson. For only a little while longer would I look up at his squarish face and see the few pale blond strands of hair that were escaping from under the brim of his hat. The touch of his tweed coat sleeve and his smell would be gone.

I could clearly picture my brother back in the familiar clean setting of the sanatorium. There he was still in a place where we both had been safe. In my head I could not form a picture of the promised nice place I was going to. It had begun to snow. I thought of the other bus ride in the night two years before. The airplanes raining exploding bombs from above. The dazed arrival on the coast of Sweden.

We were riding through a snow-covered landscape with leafless winter trees and a somber variety of pines. *Herr* Nillson pointed out various features of the Swedish cottages we passed. Some were made of gray stone. Some others of wood, often painted in the dense red of knitting yarns. *Röda stugor.* (Red cottages.) I had learned to sing a song with that title. A flagpole stood in front of every property, neat and empty. *Herr* Nillson sensed that I was puzzled.

"These are summerhouses," he explained. "People from Stockholm and elsewhere come here to fish and swim and sail. In the summertime a Swedish flag, in the shape of a long streamer, is hung in front of every house to show that the people are home and guests and neighbors are welcome to visit."

He was talking about things I could not really picture or comprehend. Oh, yes. I had gone to a place in the country in the summertime. I remembered those summers with Niania in Łapanów, with all those murky relatives, even before the Nazis came, as something squeezed and stifling. "Don't go out to the fields! You will step in cow dung." "The goats will chase you." "Don't go near the river! You'll fall in and drown." And I thought of the pails filled with muddy water and tiny dead white-bellied fish, which Niania would toss back into the river. I had no idea what it might be like to swim in fresh, clear water. To float and not choke. To welcome neighbors smilingly with waving banners. To sail in a boat. What was sailing? A picture in a book.

I smiled at *Herr* Nillson, hoping that I had put an eager enough expression on my face. Pretending to understand the images of the breezy Swedish summer world, with which he was trying to repaint this barren, scraggy coastal landscape. I tried to hide my real confusion from him. And with the confusion the fear of the daily life that was to be reshaped for me once again.

22

THE BUS CAME TO A STOP AT A WOODEN FENCE held together with an iron gate. "We have arrived." *Herr* Nillson had been saying that the trip would not be long. Yet his simple announcement made me jump out of my seat. Almost the way the concentration camp alarms and shouts used to shake my worn body into instant resigned attention. A woman who sat right behind us looked up and smiled at me. A fleeting motherly smile. She must have heard what *Herr* Nillson had been saying to me. Maybe she had sensed how I felt and was sorry for me. On her lap she was holding an illustrated magazine I recognized. I used to read it at the sanatorium. For several months I had looked forward to the weekly installments of the exciting story of Queen Kristina in exile.

I took my suitcase. *Herr* Nillson offered me his hand to help me off the bus. With the other gloved hand he gave the iron gate a slight push. With a screech of hinges it opened easily. No guards. But I couldn't pass through a gate without thinking of them.

"You will feel well here." *Herr* Nillson reassured me once again. "You will see."

Dutifully I trudged at his side. Trudged the way I had done so many times in plowed and muddy fields with my brother and Niania. Putting one foot in front of the other, I had trudged in snow and ice surrounded by Nazis. Never knowing to what or where I was trudging.

My teeth were clenched. My face could easily fold itself into surliness. I didn't want *Herr* Nillson to suspect that I no longer trusted him or anything he said. Why, why was he really taking me to this place? He could have been cleverly lying to me all along. The city was far behind. The bus had left. I heard no sounds of people anywhere. There was no one to be seen on the grounds. This whole place could be another kind of concentration camp. If I tried to run away, then what? The houses all around stood empty at this time of year. *Herr* Nillson had told me that. That might have been a clever signal. A warning not to try to run away. If I did, I could find the lady who smiled at me on the bus. Her destination must have been somewhere nearby this place called Kummelnäs. Even if I found her, then what? A friendly smile is one thing. Having a foreign runaway on your hands would be another story.

We had reached the gray stone building that was set apart from and looked more important than the wooden houses that surrounded it. *Herr* Nillson knocked on the closed door. We walked into a small room with a man sitting behind a desk. "This is . . ." *Herr* Nillson introduced me to the man, who gave his name as something ending in *ski.* His severe face tried to crease itself into a pleasant official smile. It was directed less at me than at *Herr* Nillson. The smile further thinned out the already thin line of the man's mouth. Somewhere in the corner of his curled lip I saw a glint of silvery metal. The shine of a tooth. Before it was stopped by a hedge of dark hair, *pan* (Mister) Ski's high forehead shone in the pale winter light coming through the window.

There were no questions for me to answer. I listened to *Herr* Nillson making final my transfer into this institution. With every passing moment his parting was becoming more and more real. My fears and suspicions were ebbing, giving way to sadness and resignation. I looked around the office. The Polish national emblem, a white eagle on a red background, made of cut paper, was stuck between two small Polish flags on the wall above *pan* Ski's desk. A portrait of the heroic *Marszałek* (Marshall) Piłsudski hung nearby. Polishness had been glued onto this place of exile.

On another wall, crookedly hung, was a framed oleograph of the Virgin and Child. With a guilty cramp in my chest I felt a distancing from the picture. Not because among Poles my Jewishness would be dredged out of me again, but because in the Sunday school teachings at the sanatorium I had become accustomed to the less frenzied Christianity of the Swedish Lutheran Church.

"This has all been a mistake," I wanted to hear *Herr* Nillson say. "This young lady does not belong here. She wishes to be back with the nice nurses in their blue-and-white striped uniforms and white aprons. Please tell me the time the next bus will be leaving Kummelnäs." That is not what was being said.

"So. Her mother and father will be coming," I heard instead from the man with the *ski* name. I had never heard anyone speak Swedish with a Polish accent. When I had come to the sanatorium, in my first grunting struggles, I had only thought of adding one word onto the next, like stringing beads. I thrilled with every additional morsel that led to better understanding. I never really thought of what I actually sounded like. Before I talked "like a *skånska,*" I must have talked like *pan* Ski.

"Oh, yes." There was officiousness in *Herr* Nill-son's voice. "Their Swedish visa is expected at the end of April." The two officials went on chatting and clarifying my future. *Herr* Nillson's elegant, lilting speech mingled with the hissing consonants of *pan* Ski's harsh Polish accent.

Until the conversation between the Swedish *Herr* Nillson and the Polish *pan* Something-ski, I had almost forgotten that yes, there would be a mother and a father. Yes. They had been found. From the other side of the Baltic I had had letters. Yes. I had written to them. Yes, of course. Everything was all set. They would come for me. In this sadly ceremonious little room in a stone house in the middle of a rocky coastal landscape, I could not really imagine that "mother" and "father" were anything but two more official words. In spite of all the happy letters that had been coming regularly, I did not trust that real people would come for me and carry me away to hold my hand and kiss me good-night and make me a daughter.

Herr Nillson shook hands with *pan* Ski and declined an invitation to lunch. In the next second he was shaking my hand.

"*Adjö,*" he said. "*Lycka till.* (Good-bye. Good luck.) Surely we will meet again someday." He didn't

have to say that. He didn't have to pretend that he had
any need to see me again. He had let me stay in his
home. He had given me a storybook as a present. He
had for a few hours made me forget that he was just
a Swedish official in charge of a refugee. And now he
headed for the door.

Through the window I watched him go in the
direction of the iron gate we had just walked through.
Then he passed out of my sight and was gone. I didn't
want to cry in front of *pan* Ski, who had just arranged
on his face another one of his thin-lipped smiles.

"Come with me now, Hanka," he said in Polish.

With *Herr* Nillson gone, the comfort of my adop-
tive Swedishness was fast blurring and fading away.
I felt as if I had been recaptured and retied to Poland
with invisible ropes. Carrying my little suitcase, I
followed *pan* Ski toward one of the larger wooden
buildings not far from his office.

When we walked into the hall with long tables,
I knew at once why there had been no one on the
grounds. It was noon. Through the clatter of dishes I
heard shouts and gusts of conversation in Polish. Polish. How long the "Shelter for Polish Young People"
had been here I didn't know. But surely, long before
I arrived, these Polish kids had been eating meals
together. And at night they had been whispering
together before going to sleep. Long before I arrived,

they had had time to form an intimate, comfortable clump. Just because I, too, had once lived in Poland, it would be expected of me to pretend to belong.

"This is Hanka." *Pan* Ski had directed me toward one of the tables. "She will stay with us for a while."

All through the bus ride by *Herr* Nillson's side, I had felt as if I were being put away. Suddenly in the midst of this Polish noise, being presented as someone who would only be "with us for a while" made me into a visitor. A guest. Someone just stopping by to wait for her mother and father to arrive. I put down my suitcase.

Pan Ski, his duties done, nodded and walked away to have his lunch at another table. One of the boys moved over, making a space for me to sit down next to him on the bench. *"Servus,"* he mumbled. Three girls threw other greetings at me in Polish. Again I was reminded that for the present Swedish had to be tucked away. "Jasiek," the boy introduced himself. He must have been eighteen or nineteen. All of them had stopped eating for a moment. Hands reached to shake mine. The boy sitting on the other side of the table said, "I am Stefan." He seemed a little younger than Jasiek. Both boys had thin dirty blond hair. Jasiek's face and neck were covered with pimples. I thought of the boils my leg had been covered with that summer in Łapanów. The girls were Dana and Sabina and

Marysia. All three had limp, short hair, in various shades of pale brown. Where had they all come from? Had they been in a concentration camp?

I was hungry. I inhaled the smell of the thick soup in the bowl before me. My twitch of fresh confidence mingled with the aroma of food. I dipped my spoon and tasted. The old familiar taste surprised me.

When I had first been brought to the sanatorium, in those first few weeks out of the concentration camp, the girls in the ward got into the habit of letting me finish whatever scraps of food were left on their plates. I was a strange, hungry animal in their midst. If they laughed at me, I didn't care. After almost two years of plenty I had lost the memory of the sucking feeling in an empty belly. I had begun to tire of the Swedish fish dishes that were often smothered in egg and cream sauces. And the worst was *lutfisk*. Even the thought of it gagged me. At Christmas it was a tradition. We were supposed to eat it all up. Or we would not be allowed the ham and rice pudding that followed.

The Polish soup was delicious. Potatoes and barley and mushrooms mixed together. Full of flour and flavoring. Thick and fragrant. A taste from before the war. And even from those times during the war when Niania got enough ingredients to make a soup in the country. Or in the city when we lined up with our bowls at the convent soup kitchen.

I looked into the familiar flatness of the faces around me. They were rough country faces, reminding me of so many people from our wanderings with Niania. Only one of the girls could be thought pretty. She had blue eyes, a straight, small nose, and a graceful neck. When she laughed, I saw that her teeth were as uneven as mine. All of us had crooked teeth. No one at the table was as dark as I was. I would have to make sure that they would see the holy medals around my neck. I would prove to them that I was not a real *Żydówka* (Jewess). For the moment I put a lid on my fear and suspicion of this Polish no-man's-land. And I concentrated on spooning the shamelessly thick, good Polish soup into my mouth.

23

THE DIRECTORS WHO RAN THE CAMP HAD TRIED to organize study. A couple of the cottages had been transformed into classrooms. We sat at tables and had lessons in Polish grammar, writing, and Polish history. Although I had never gone to one, none of this felt like real school. There were attempts at crafts instruction. I remember cutting out gold and red and white pieces of paper from a pattern to paste together a Polish eagle. Like the one I had seen on the wall in *pan* Ski's office the day I had arrived with *Herr* Nillson. I didn't do it well. I missed the embroidery and Sunday school lessons I had had at the sanatorium.

Sometimes in the evenings we gathered in the big hall, and one of the directors would read aloud. There was a severe-looking lady with a pointed nose and tight gray hair who insisted that we all call her Mother. She read in Polish from a book called *Huckleberry Finn*. I didn't pay much attention to the story. The curious name *Dżim* kept popping out of "Mother's" reading over and over again.

I shared a room with the three girls I had met in the dining hall the day I arrived. In one corner they had set up a little shrine with the statue of the Virgin. They must have suspected that I was Jewish, but I knew all the prayers and litanies as well as they did. We prayed and recited the rosary together. Whatever they may have thought, I proved to them that I was a Catholic, and they left it at that. The girls were older than I was. They talked about the boys and getting married and jobs they would get when they left for America or Canada. I did not think of asking them about what had happened to their parents or how they had come to Sweden.

At night the girls told scary stories, not unlike those I had heard from Niania or the women in her village. One terrible thing had happened right there at the camp not long before I came. A boy had gone skating and had fallen through the thin ice of a nearby pond. It was dark. No one had been able to get to him in time. The boy had drowned. Sometimes when I had to walk by the pond, I imagined screams for help. I imagined his dripping, frozen body being carried back to one of the cottages. Had he been laid out on his bed overnight while the other boys slept? Silent, with nose pointing at the ceiling. The way Krysia had been laid on the bed across the aisle from me in the convent dormitory.

There was one other Jewish girl at the camp. She was a funny-looking girl with small eyes and bright, shiny red cheeks. She lived in another cottage. Her name was Ryfka. The Polish kids never stopped calling her *Żydówka, Żydówka.* They played tricks on her. They sneaked into her room and messed up her bed. They threw her things out of the window. She never complained and always met all the taunting with a silly, humble smile on her face. Because there was Ryfka to pick on, I was spared. Ryfka tried to be friends with me, but I avoided her as much as possible. I knew she was just waiting patiently until she could leave and go to Palestine. I didn't understand why she so eagerly hung on to being Jewish. I just wanted to get away and begin to be with Swedish people.

Very early one morning, on the second day of Easter that spring, I woke in a drenching shower of freezing water. Some boys had managed to sneak into our cottage to play an old Polish countryside prank and had emptied buckets of water on us still asleep in our beds. Another time I woke up, choking, to the smell of smoke. The whole camp was awakened. We wrapped ourselves in whatever coverings we could grab and ran out and stood frightened and shivering on the grounds. A fire had erupted somewhere under one of the wooden cottages. It had spread, but no one was hurt. How exactly the fire had started was never discovered. For a long time after that night the blankets on our cots and our clothes stank, and I walked around with a sick, burning taste in my mouth.

In Kraków Mother and Father were making arrangements to come to Sweden. Letters with Polish postage stamps on the envelopes were crossing the Baltic and were delivered to *pan* Ski's office. I thought about how frightening and difficult it had been for Niania to contact Mother during the war. How we had not heard a word from Father in all those years. Only a short time had passed since none of us knew if anybody we wanted to be in touch with was even alive. Now thin pieces of paper full of continued jubilation about our survival were delivered into my hands. But there were also worries. Mostly about not knowing the new language. Proudly I wrote, "Dearest Mamusiu and Tatusiu and Nianiusiu, don't worry. I speak Swedish well." After all it was my letter written in Swedish that had led to the locating of Niania and Mother in Kraków. "I will help translate." I licked the envelope and put a Swedish stamp on it. The letter would get to Poland. And no German could stop it.

A letter came from Niania. A long, loving letter saying how much she missed her little Hanusia. She was sorry, but now that the Germans were gone, she did not wish to leave Poland. Her headaches were worse. She constantly needed her *Kogutki*. She did not want to travel far away. I wrote to tell her that in Sweden there were wonderful nurses and doctors and headache powders.

In her next letter, filled with the usual loving words, Niania wrote, "I have heard that there are carvings with the image of the Virgin at the entrance of every church. People step on her Holy Image as they go in." Who had told Niania such awful things? Of course I had only Sunday school lessons in my room from the kind nurses. I had never gone into a church outside the sanatorium. How could I convince Niania that Sweden was a wonderful country and its people were kind and very devoted Christians? I hoped that Mother and Father could talk her into changing her mind. That living with us would be more important to Niania than her fears of the Lutherans.

The next letter from Mother told me that Niania no longer lived with them in Kraków. She had decided to go to live with a sister, whom she had not seen for many years. I had never known that Niania had a sister.

Could people still drop away and disappear the way they had before the Nazis had been defeated? I had had two years of food and shelter and quiet care from kind people. Now I was not certain how I felt about Niania not wanting to be with me again. Not certain how I felt about anybody from the times before my life had become peaceful in Sweden.

One evening at dinnertime *pan* Ski ushered my mother and father into the big hall. All around, the kids paused in their eating and stared. I stood up stiff and nervous, mumbling, "Mama . . . uhh, *pani—*" I got lost. Didn't know how to continue properly the introduction of this couple to the kids at my table. Coming face-to-face with Mother was not so odd. Only a couple of years had passed since I had last seen her. But Father? Before me stood a slightly familiar short stranger. The elegant gray streak that used to cut through his hair on a diagonal from forehead to the back of his head had blended with the rest of his completely gray hair. He wore a long rough leather coat and clumsy, heavy boots that were quite worn but nicely polished. I tried to stop shaking, to act normal. I was almost as tall as this new older man, whom I had known when I was so little, as my *tatuś*. He reached his arms out to me. In his tentative embrace I felt the strangeness of the much larger volume of daughter I had become in seven years of separation. His smell was familiar and nice.

The two boys sitting next to me got up from their seats and asked Mother and Father to sit down. Plates were put in front of them. There I sat, surrounded by my Polish camp companions and the smell of cabbage and sausage and garlic, staring at my plate, thinking of the day *Herr* Nillson had dropped me here and walked away. I cast quick glances at this couple who were my parents. I arranged and rearranged myself on the bench, trying to live up to the joy of this event. Would any of my camp mates have parents who would come for them? Between polite bits of conversation, mostly instigated by Mother, we took bites of the food on our plates.

After dinner I showed my parents the room I lived in, and we walked on the grounds. The light was turning toward spring, and there was a beautiful glow in the evening sky. It was still cold, but the snow was gone. Toward the end of winter I had learned how to ski. On the polished wooden boards strapped to my shoes, placing one foot in front of the other, I had been able to get away quietly to the outskirts of the camp and go gliding on snow in nearby woods and fields and even slide down an occasional small slope. I remembered how before the war Father used to go skiing in the Polish winter resort Zakopane. "I know how to ski," I said shyly to my father. "I hope you are careful, Hanusiu," my mother said. Careful? What danger was there in pushing myself on a couple of boards along snowy ground in a quiet, peaceful woods?

In the dining hall later that evening a dance had been organized. Tables were moved, and benches placed against the wall. Recorded Polish music played on a phonograph. Some of the girls danced with one another. I had collected several dresses that had come in a package from a Swedish relief agency. I kept running back to my room to change from one dress to another to show my parents how nice and grown-up I looked. The third time I ran back, I changed into a red dress with a flounced capelet that was too big on me.

"Stop running in and out so much, Hanusiu!" My mother looked uncomfortably around the hall. "You'll catch a cold." Then, smoothing my hair, she said, "I think we should arrange to cut your hair. You would look prettier with short hair." Before the war my hair had always been worn in a polite short haircut parted on the side and caught with a big ribbon or a barrette. That was the way Mother and Father liked it. Niania preferred braids. Once the war started and Niania was completely in charge of me, she let me grow my hair. How could my mother say such a thing about my hair now? Didn't she know about the shaved heads in concentration camps? Couldn't she guess that once my hair grew out I never wanted to cut it again? Or did she think of me as if I were still four or five years old? Why hadn't Niania come?

24

I FELT SPECIAL WHEN I SAID GOOD-BYE TO MY
roommates, good-bye to *pan* Ski and "Mother," good-
bye to the awful boys and the grounds and cottages.
I had no wish to see any of these people ever again.
I shook Ryfka's hand. Before I turned to walk away
with my suitcase and a mother and a father, I saw in
her funny little face a shadow of sadness mixed with
envy. Why had I not tried to be nicer to her? I wondered how much longer she would have to endure this
Polish holding tank before she was allowed to emigrate to Palestine.

My first days in Stockholm were spent leading
my whispering, demanding mother and father to
agency after agency in charge of official papers for
newly arrived immigrants. Timid and self-conscious,

I was afraid of making mistakes when translating from Swedish to Polish and back again. I thought of my lucky brother still at the sanatorium, probably wrapped in a cozy blanket on one of the veranda chairs, drinking hot chocolate, dozing, reading. I had imagined and longed for the wonderful life I would finally have as a child of parents who would take care of me. Instead, depended on as negotiator and guide, I was the one who had to take care of them. I wished *Herr* Nillson would appear from somewhere to help me out.

My parents had found lodgings in a boardinghouse. A *pensionat,* it was called. It was on a nice square not far from one of the many harbors on Mälaren (Lake Mälar), the lake that surrounds the several islands that make up the various boroughs of the city of Stockholm. *Fröken* (Miss) Löwengård, the landlady, haltingly spoke enough German to be able to communicate with her boarders, who, like my parents, were recent Jewish arrivals from Poland. If German didn't work, I was called on to help with translating.

Our room in the *pensionat* was big enough to contain a largish bed for my parents, a narrow cot for me, a washstand, and a wardrobe for clothes. There was a window looking out on a courtyard. Down the hall were a communal toilet and a bathroom with a tub. My parents had brought the few possessions they had gathered together after the war. My father's suitcase looked very, very old. He had brought it from Russia. It was made of heavy brown leather with steel fittings. They had bought a sewing machine in Poland. It was big and had an ornate pedal pump. It stayed quietly in a corner, taking up space, until a couple of years later, when in high school I learned how to make my own clothes and began to use it regularly.

Fröken Löwengård, the landlady, lived in her own section of the *pensionat* with a painter. She ran her establishment smoothly. Rooms were simple but spotless. Meals were served on time twice a day in a paneled dining room. Tables were neatly set with tablecloths and napkins. I was well used to the Swedish fish and egg dishes and cheeses that had stilled my hunger and made me well. The group of survivors, sitting three or four at a table, spent a lot of time griping about the strange foods they didn't like. Not even bothering to lower their voices, they grumbled in Polish about everything. The rooms were too small or too dark. There was not enough hot water. They didn't like the painter's pictures, which hung on the walls of the hallways and the dining room. They found fault with the landlady's eye makeup, her tinted hair. Among the other complaints I heard coming in a constant stream from the refugees and my parents was "She isn't even married to him!"

From the landlady's private little sitting room piano music was often heard. Mostly jazz. "Ach," I heard my mother sigh. "Why never a note of Chopin?" The sound of any kind of music on the piano wafting through a window was comforting to me. Mixed with traffic noises, it was a beautiful proof that at last I had started living life in a civilized city again.

I thought *Fröken* Löwengård looked like a movie star. I liked the artist's paintings of flowers in vases, of bowls of fruit, wine bottles, naked ladies. The colors were so pretty. And they looked so real. In the dining room I would overhear snatches of conversations about theater and art between the landlady and the painter and their friends. Talk that the foreigners surrounding me could not understand. Compared with this interesting Swedish couple, the lodgers made me think of the poor relatives from Łapanów. I was ashamed to be part of this group. I was disappointed in the way my parents willingly joined in the discontented Polish murmurings. I was sad that they could not converse elegantly in Swedish.

My father found a job. He went off one morning dressed in a suit and tie and hat. He looked almost the way I had remembered him from before the war. When he was *mój tatuś* and much taller than I and the gray in his hair had only been that interesting streak.

In the evening my father came home from his new job and began to cry. Mother had told me how he had cried the night he kissed me good-bye before he left to evade the Nazis. But I had been asleep in my bed under Niania's protective angel picture. I had never seen my father cry.

"I can't do this," he sobbed. "I can't do this!" His first job in Stockholm was that of an elevator man in an office building. He had had to change into a uniform and a cap. All day he had tried to be polite and servile to people whose language he did not understand. All day he had looked at well-dressed businesspeople getting on and off the elevator, going to their offices. "Before the Nazis robbed me, I had my own factory," my father cried. "Now I am nothing!" Even in Siberia he had had his own stand at a bazaar where he sold sweets and trinkets. "In this country I am nothing!" he went on and on. "Nothing."

I had lost nothing I had cared about. I had only vague memories of having things that belonged to me before the war. I had become used to not having books or toys or pretty clothes or friends. I had been without these things for so long I didn't really know how to miss what I had never had. I was starting my life in a beautiful city with neon lights and church bells and movie theaters and a blue sky. I had learned to speak a language that felt good on my tongue and sounded beautiful in my ears. I had a clean body. I had hair. I was new.

I had been without my big, good-smelling father for so many years. But now I was ready for this smaller found father to take charge and to take care of me. I could not understand why it was not enough for him just to have survived and to have his wife and children back. And to be alive in a country where there was plenty of food and where people were quietly helpful to strangers and the hating of Jews was not their main purpose in life.

My father quit the elevator job and found work in a factory that manufactured men's suits. He liked it better and didn't cry when he came home from work. Mother, too, got a job. In a plant that produced sanitary napkins. More patient and docile than Father, she spent all day stuffing wads of cotton into oblong gauze casings and tying their ends.

My parents found a Polish dressmaker, another recent arrival. I was measured for a new outfit. It would be my first new piece of clothing since before the war. Mother and father decided I should have a navy middy dress, pleated skirt and top with sailor collar and white piping. They liked the look of a girls'-school uniform remembered from times past. When the outfit was finished, I went with my father to a big department store to shop for shoes. I stepped into a pair of sandals. So new and white and shiny with a pretty buckle and straps! I looked at my feet in the low mirror and took a few small steps back and forth on the carpeted floor. From my toes through the soles of my feet my whole body was filled with new hope and promise. The sun was shining, the tramways were clanking, and the war was over. I was a daughter. I had a father. He was buying new shoes for me.

The saleswoman carefully enunciated the price. And then I heard my father say in German, *"Kann es nicht ein bisschen billiger sein?"* ("Can't you make it a little cheaper?") My bliss was punctured like a rubber balloon. Again feeling like the hairless dark monkey the first day at the sanatorium, I wanted to be lifted out of the white sandals and evaporate from shame. The saleslady understood and was taken aback by my father's unexpected and gauche foreign question. She attempted a prim smile. Then she pinched her lips and simply shook her head. Didn't my father know that in this country in an elegant store people did not haggle about price like traders on the black market in Poland or Russia? Why did he have to betray me by becoming an old Jewish peddler in a Stockholm department store? I would rather not have the sandals. With my bent head I sat down and quietly slipped them off.

My father took out his small worn wallet and counted out Swedish *kronor* and paid for the sandals. The saleslady put them in a box. She put the box in a paper bag. She handed the package to me. When at another counter we picked out some white knee socks, my father did not question the price. I breathed more easily once we were out on the street again.

Summers in Sweden are beautiful. The sun shines until almost midnight, disappears for a couple of hours, and rises again. We waited for word of my brother's recovery and settled into life. We went for walks, boat rides, to look at pictures in museums. In a photograph taken on the square in front of the Parliament building I am wearing my new dress, the white socks and sandals. There are white ribbons in my braids. I stand between my mother and my father. My tall mother wears a well-cut, square-shouldered suit and a fedora. My father is hatless, his wavy gray hair slicked down. He has casually put a hand in his jacket pocket. I am almost as tall as my father. We have survived the war. We pose, Sunday best, smiling and confident. In the photograph I am the child of parents again.

When later that summer my brother was completely well, we asked *Fröken* Löwengård for a larger room in the *pensionat*. One did become available. The new room had its own sink with running water. It had an extra sleeping alcove with two cots. My parents went on the train to get my brother at the sanatorium.

"I don't know the man," my brother whispered to me when he came. "I don't remember having a father." Had Tatuś kissed him the night he cried when he left? Mother never said. My brother was startled by the city and confused by life with these people called parents. I was tired of the refugee group in the *pensionat* without anyone my own age. I was happy to have my brother back in my life.

At last, for the first time in my life, I sat at a desk in a real classroom. I loved going to school. I loved everything about it. Getting out of bed and dressing for school! The weight of my satchel that held my books and notebooks, pencils, and pens with nibs. The clanking of the tramway on the short ride from the boardinghouse. I loved slipping into the old scratched-up little wooden desk and laying out books and copybooks. Classes were strict. We snapped to attention every morning to greet the teacher in unison. I loved the thin, severe, tall schoolmistress, whose hair was cut short and clasped to one side with a barrette. She wore tweed skirts and prim blouses and gray sweaters. There was a prayer and the singing of a psalm. I dipped my pen in the inkwell that nested in a little round hole in an indented trough in the desk and wrote in my exercise book. I had a blotter to dry the writing. The books I had been given—history of Sweden, grammar, arithmetic books, geography—had doodles and scribbles that previous students had put there. Homework was not a chore. I knew it backward and forward. When we settled in for the various periods of the day, my hand was constantly in the air. I pounced on the groaning board of words, of history dates, of stories, of poems, of the columns of sums to be calculated. We had music instruction, too. Stories of the lives of famous composers. And we sang. It didn't matter what we were learning. I questioned nothing. My eager brain feasted on the lessons in the books the way my tattered hungry stomach had feasted on the canned beans and Spam from the Care packages.

The trouble with school was the sports and gymnastics classes. Several times a week we changed into shorts and shirts and went to the gym hall, which was full of highly polished wood and smelled of rubber and shellac. There were exercises on a wooden crossbeam. My classmates easily went through a routine that required one to grab onto the beam from below, then swing the legs over the head and balance with arms straight. It was a kind of somersault. There was another exercise on a contraption that stood on four legs. We lined up and ran toward it. Grabbing on to a handle on each side on top, we were to spread our legs and jump swiftly onto a mat on the other side. Or we were to hang upside down from ladderlike structures. My hands got sweaty. I could hardly get hold of the polished beam. Swinging my legs over my head was impossible. I never could work up a sufficient amount of speed and energy to jump over the four-legged contraption. I was ashamed of being so terribly clumsy. Every time it was my turn to run or jump or climb, I felt as if a black witch called Terrible Fear lived somewhere deep, deep inside me and was always ready with a rope to tie my limbs, squash whatever courage I may have had, and cackle with delight at my shame.

We had outings to a skating rink. Skates were provided to those who didn't have their own. They were the kinds of skates that were strapped and fastened over one's shoes. Several girls wore beautiful short skirts and white skating boots. Their laughter and joking kept me at a distance once again. My classmates were gliding and swirling with ease and grace while I was terrified of even stepping onto the treacherous expanse of smooth ice. My legs were two wobbly rigid poles that would not obey the demands of the steel blades way down under my feet. My ankles caved in. I hung desperately on to the side rail and tried to disappear into corners of the rink.

Being so clumsy at sports, and such a good girl in the classroom, distanced me from my classmates. Not many kids came forward to be my friends. And I continued to be singled out as a stranger. Not everyone in Sweden was blond, but almost never did one see a girl with dark braids and my olive-skinned Gypsy look. People turned to look at me on the street. I often heard passersby call out or mumble under their breath, *"Neger! Neger!"* ("Negro! Negro!") Or "Indian." Not so much expressions of malice and hatred as astonishment at seeing someone so unexpectedly swarthy in Nordic Stockholm. I felt surprised, singled out, ashamed.

Still, there was a difference between the me on my first days at school and the me I had been during my first days at the sanatorium. I could read, and I could speak. Quietly, timidly, I was prepared to pave my way into my new country. Being pointed out as an oddity did not translate into threat and danger. Not the way it had in Poland. There, even before the Nazis came, being called *"Żydówka! Żydówka!"* wasn't just a tease.

25

NOT EVERYONE IN SWEDEN WAS REQUIRED TO go to what was called a *realskola* (high school). I took an entrance test, along with many of my classmates. Not all of them got in. My scores were fine. My teacher beamed. My parents were proud. On my first day of *realskola* I was scared and excited but better prepared than I had been a year earlier. In the new school I was one of many students starting from scratch.

In my new school boys and girls attended classes together. The boys were pimply and rough and never stopped teasing one another and the girls. I was surprised when in the schoolyard I found myself included with cliques of girls, giggling and whispering in mock disapproval of the boys. I was relieved that during the all-important gym and sports periods girls and boys were separated into different sections. I dreaded it all still.

Different teachers came to the classroom to teach geography and history and Swedish literature, algebra and geometry. We began to study English. German was required. In the mouths of my Swedish teachers and classmates the language that had spelled such dread for so many years gradually took on the simple demand of a skill to be memorized and shaped and conquered. I recognized German as the distant relative of the Swedish that I cherished. And in the words of songs that we sometimes sang the language revealed its beauty. German never stopped echoing the power of an enemy, but it had become approachable as another subject for schoolwork. Guardedly and obediently I excelled in it.

English was the language I knew from the movies. It was the language of cowboys and beautiful men and women who danced in glittering costumes and sang and smiled, showing great big, brilliant rows of straight white teeth. Or the speech of people who, accompanied by jazz music, moved in shadowy black-and-white interiors or lurked on treacherous dark city streets. English was the language of the songs my two best girlfriends and I learned from records and from the radio and that we sang loudly, drawing attention to ourselves as we marched arm in arm on Stockholm streets. English was an imp and a trickster. It required contortions of tongue and mouth to make words that didn't quite resemble their letters when written down on the page. And I loved the sound and the look of it.

In my new school one morning the art teacher, a cheerful woman dressed in a colorful smock, with beautiful pale, pale blond hair coiled in a thick bun, came in and said, "Today we are going to learn something about observation and the use of *akvareller.*" Even though it was a perfectly normal Swedish word that meant "watercolors," it was not one the boys in the class used in their daily conversations. They started to snicker and make funny remarks and elbow one another.

We gathered by the blackboard around *fru* (Mrs.) Malmkvist's big desk. She opened a portfolio and spread out colored prints of elegant rooms depicting tables with vases of flowers, sofas, and chairs. The boys let it be known that they would have preferred pictures of ears and pinup girls.

"Next week." *Fru* Malmkvist was unruffled. "Today choose a picture of one thing you want to render, and let's get started."

Without much enthusiasm, just wanting to be obedient, I looked over the pictures carefully. My eyes fell on a print of a pretty, delicate chair. "Armchair 18th century" was printed underneath the picture. The grayish white wooden frame had a delicate cluster of carved flowers in the center on top. The same motif was repeated at the end of the curved arm supports. The seat and the oval back were upholstered in a silky fabric in blue and white stripes. I knew I had seen a chair exactly like this once before. The chair in the print looked just like the one I had been ashamed to sit down on in *Herr* Nillson's apartment!

My desk was in the back of the classroom near the window. October light was falling on the empty piece of nice art paper that *fru* Malmkvist had given me. Brand-new watercolor patties in a flat tin box, two brushes, a pencil, and a pink eraser were waiting for me. I was nervous and excited when I stepped out into the hallway to fill a little tin can with water from the sink. Amid the sounds of pencils scratching, erasers rubbing, and brushes dipping, the grumbling from the boys had quieted down.

I held the pencil in my hand and lightly and carefully sketched the outlines of the chair. I dipped my brush in the water and then rubbed it gently into one square blue color patty in the tin box. There were several shades of blue nesting side by side. I started with one blue and then blended a slightly different blue shade into the brush. I saw some green in the blue stripes and worked in a drop of color from the green watercolor patty. Where the upholstery was stretched and curved toward the frame of the chair, the colors grew subtly darker. In the rounded center they turned lighter and brighter. My brush dipped and caressed and tickled and wandered within my penciled outlines. I felt as if I were a little insect, a fly or a spider, taking a slow, careful walk up and down along the stripes, trailing, judging, matching and translating the quiet pale colors of the chair in the print to the chair in my drawing.

"That is very, very good." I was startled by *fru* Malmkvist's voice by my side. Hearing only the soft swish of the brush on paper and its tinkling against the tin can as I had dipped it in the water, I had concentrated and rendered, almost completely forgetting the teacher and my classmates.

"You don't have to work on your picture anymore," the art teacher said, smiling. "It is fine just the way it is. Look, everybody! A very good example of careful observation and a nice use of watercolors."

All around my classmates stopped pushing their pencils and brushes and looked up from their desks. *Fru* Malmkvist leaned my picture against the blackboard right next to the print. Even from a distance everyone could see that it was a picture of a blue and white striped chair faithfully copied from the old

print placed right next to it. I had even put in the
slight shadow that the chair cast on the floor underneath. From my classmates came whispers of genuine
admiration. After that morning I never wanted to live
without such murmurs.

Becoming singled out, designated as the class "artist," softened the stigma of my clumsiness in gym and
sports. Gradually even there my self-consciousness
eased. After much choking and tension in the water
of the Olympic pool that we went to several times
a month, I learned to swim. I ran the one-hundred-
meter dash. I even did some pole vaulting. I was the
goalie on the girls' soccer team.

Once a week I began to go to evening classes in a
real art school and made charcoal drawings of broken
old plaster-cast statues. Hands and feet were hard. At
home I drew portraits of my father, of my mother,
of my brother. I drew arrangements of flowers in a
vase, of fruit in a bowl, of cups and bottles standing
on tablecloths, of chairs standing empty around a
table. I painted pictures of the houses across the street
and imaginary landscapes of mountains and trees. I
looked at pictures in magazines and painted and drew
people in costumes.

Sometimes the whole class went with *fru* Malmkvist to the art museum. When I looked at paintings

then, I was not content to remain an admirer. I became the hungry wanderer and intruder into the outlines of lace on a wrist, into eyes and noses and hair, a traveler among trees and mountains against cloudy skies, a chiseler of shapes of flower petals and of the human body. I was a conspirator and a thief. I was an artist.

26

"NIANIA IS DEAD!" MOTHER CRIED OUT, READING the letter that had just come from Poland. "The poor woman! A brain tumor. My God." All those head-aches that would not go away no matter how many *Kogutki* powders my brother and I brought her. It had been a brain tumor all along. "Ach!" Mother kept sighing. "The poor woman!"

Not long before this letter a box had arrived from Poland, with a present from Niania for my birthday. My birthday, which had never been mentioned during the war. In Poland only Jewish people celebrated birthdays. Catholics had saint's days. Cutting away the string and the outer layers of brown wrapping paper, I had pulled out a fancy box and removed the lid.

From frothy tissue paper, I had lifted a large doll that reached stiff arms out to me. Her eyes opened with a snap and fixed me with a blue-gray glassy stare. The doll was dressed in a pale blue dress of soft, shiny silk with a white organdy collar with a lace trim. Her arms and legs moved, and she had a mass of hair parted in the middle that looked human. Not since before the war had I seen such an extravagant toy. And it was so big! The dolls I remember playing with once had been much, much smaller. At the time I was hiding the matzos from the Nazis that Passover morning in Łapanów, the dolls in my carriage had been old and ragged, their dresses in shreds. Once we had moved on to Niania's village, we didn't carry much with us from place to place. I don't know what had happened to my old dolls or to their carriage.

Arranging the tissue paper carefully around it, I had put the doll back in the box and replaced the lid. In my letter I had thanked Niania profusely for the *śliczna laleczka!* (gorgeous doll). I had said nothing about being too big and too embarrassed to play with dolls anymore. But when I was alone, I sometimes took the doll out of her box and tissue paper and rocked her in my arms, smoothing and rearranging her dress, adjusting her little socks and ballerina shoes.

We now lived in a small ramshackle cottage on the periphery of Stockholm. We had moved from the boarding house shortly after my brother had come out of the sanatorium. I sat on my bed in the little room I shared with my mother, listening to her sighing over the letter from Niania's sister. I took the lid off the box that held the doll. With her arms stretched rigidly before her, the doll seemed to be asking to be lifted out. The last time I had seen Niania, her outstretched arms were throwing my brother's and my coats and scarves toward us into the canvas truck, seconds before the Nazis drove us away from the convent that Christmas morning. Then the shrinking figure of Niania, wringing her hands, had disappeared from sight. Her cries, "Don't take my children! Don't hurt my little children!," fading away in the distance.

I thought of the dream Niania had had just before her mother died. From an open grave her mother had reached out her arms toward Niania. Looking at my doll in the box, I felt as if I were staring at a stiff, dead body. I slid the box from its upright position and laid it flat on the bed so that the eyes would stay closed and not stare. If I could, I would have bent the arms and crossed them on her chest. But the doll's arms did not bend that way. They only moved up and down in their sockets. from a little pouch I kept under my bed I took out my rosary. I kept it with the medals that I no longer wore around my neck.

"It is not right for you to wear those things," my mother had complained one day. "You are embarrassing us." We were still living at the *pensionat*. My parents were afraid that the other Jewish refugees might discover that their daughter walked around wearing Catholic medals around her neck. I gave in. I put my medals away.

Now I took out my rosary and wrapped it around the outstretched hands and rigid fingers of my doll. My mother, paying no attention to my fiddling, handed me the letter. I glanced at it quickly. There were simple details about the funeral. "This was a saintly and humble servant of Christ and the Virgin," the priest had said about Niania. There was a description of the grave site and the flowers. I gave the letter back to my mother and said nothing. My *niania* was dead. I would never see her again. I put the lid back and slipped the box under the bed.

I didn't cry. I was angry. Why had Niania been so stubborn?

I went into the other little room in the cottage. My brother was working on his Hebrew homework. My father had found a refugee rabbi somewhere to prepare his son for his bar mitzvah. Once a week he came to the house and spread his books on the round table that my mother had covered with a blue oilcloth and gave my brother lessons.

"Why didn't Niania want to come and live with us?" I said to my brother.

"I don't know," he said calmly, not looking up from his work. "Maybe as soon we were gone, she didn't love us anymore!"

"Oh, you are so stupid!" I was ready to slam his smug face into his book. "You don't care about her because she didn't come for us when we were deported." My brother said nothing. "She loved me more than you anyway!" I shouted.

I didn't want to fight with my brother. He was confused enough. Coming out of the sanatorium, living with parents he hardly knew. Especially a father he had no memory of at all. None. He was starting school for the first time in a city that was totally new to him. Here he was obediently working on words in yet another language from a book that opened backward. How was he supposed to know what Niania felt or thought? Or if she died only because she had decided not to leave Poland? "I am sorry," I said. "I am sorry." I was. I was sorry for Niania, for my brother, for me. Outside, it was dark. No leaves on the trees. November. I was sorry about everything.

The more I thought about it, the more I was

convinced that if Niania had come, she would have been cured of her brain tumor. I had been sick with tuberculosis. My brother had been sick with tuberculosis. In Sweden we had been made well again. In Poland, from the same sickness, Krysia had died. In Poland everybody ended up laid out, with noses and feet pointing to the ceiling.

Maybe it was my fault. During the last year, whenever a letter had come from Niania, mother had to remind me, often even nag me to write back. When I finally wrote, maybe my letters had not been nice enough. Maybe Niania had suspected that Hanusia was forgetting to be her loyal Catholic-Jewish girl. Or had she finally decided not to have anything more to do with Jews? Or maybe my parents, remembering all those fights with Niania from before the war, didn't try very hard to convince her to come.

Mother and Father were constantly reminding me how important it was to be Jewish. "You should be proud," my mother repeated again and again. It became a command. They had made me obtain permission to stay out of school for the Jewish New Year. I went along with my parents to Stockholm's one temple a few times. It meant nothing to me. Soon I was able to find excuses and managed to slip out of going.

I was almost fifteen years old. I was learning things, reading books and painting and drawing pictures. I went to piano concerts and plays and hugged the walls of dance halls, trembling for the moment some boy would come toward me and put his arm around me and I would follow him onto the shiny floor to do a fox-trot or waltz or jitterbug. At last I had friends. I wanted to belong to them, to their world. To the world that allowed me to breathe better in every way than I could before. I did not want to be claimed by loyalties and duties that pulled me back toward the darkness in my life.

On Sundays I sang in the alto section in *Söderkyrkan's* choir. The music teacher at my school was the South Church's choir director. My parents could not object because I said it was part of the music program. It was an honor to have been chosen along with three other girls from my class.

In *Söderkyrkan* not long after Niania's death we performed Mozart's Requiem Mass. When I opened my throat to blend my voice with the others and the notes and melodies and harmonies wove and rose high to the rafters and spilled into corners of the great church, my parents' nagging about being Jewish, Niania's old distrusts and belief that Lutherans trampled on the image of the Holy Mother dissolved and evaporated into nothingness. Bathed in the glow of candles and winter light filtering through stained glass windows, with organ pipes roaring behind our voices, I let flow into my singing my own sadness, my own private, secret thoughts. "Dear heaven, let my poor Nianiusia rest in eternal peace." Not making the sign of the cross, not twisting a rosary, far away from *kościół Mariacki,* from Kraków, from Poland, I was a teenaged girl in a house of God in Stockholm, Sweden, singing a last good-bye to my dear, difficult Niania, whom I would never, ever see again.

In Stockholm, Sweden, I was sixteen years old when my parents announced that our American visas were ready. We were shortly to pack up and leave. I felt betrayed. While I had taken root, my parents had thought of Sweden only as a stopping place before going to America. My brother was on their side. I could not understand why the three of them would not want to stay right where we were forever. I protested and cried and raged. I had no wish to tear myself away from friends and studies, the graceful familiarity of the city I had grown to love, the language that danced easily on my tongue, once again to be tossed into exile.

At Central Station, where on a dark winter morning five years earlier I had arrived in Stockholm for the first time with *Herr* Nillson, I had to say my tearful farewells to my friends, my teachers, and my first boyfriend. I promised to come back. They promised to write. We all promised, promised. As the train that would carry me to the coast pulled away from the platform, the clump of waving Swedish people who had come to see me leave grew smaller and smaller and vanished from sight. On the train, against my mother's objections, I opened the window and let the icy wind whip away the tears on my face.

Later that day, with our belongings stashed in the bowels of the old liner, we sailed away. The foggy, wintry coast of western Sweden shrank in the distance, and I tried to believe that I had not said good-bye for always.

After two weeks of a stormy crossing we stood on deck in winter morning sunlight, sailing past the Statue of Liberty, into the picture postcard of the shimmering skyline of the great city. My chest constricted with brand-new promises and fears. My mind was clogged with rehearsed phrases in English and with vague images of what life there among the tall buildings and unfamiliar streets would bring. Entered on the appropriate line in my passport, right under my picture stamped with a seal was my identity. *Affärselev,* or Business Student. For the

purpose of immigration my parents had thought
that a less suspect goal than "student of art."

With the neatly arranged evidence of my new, ques-
tionably useful skills filed in a cardboard portfolio tied
with strings, I was arriving in New York City.

EPILOGUE

MANY YEARS HAD PASSED WHEN MY BROTHER, an American professor of psychology, traveled to Poland for the first time since the end of the war. He was able to piece together details of how on a dark January night a ten-year-old girl and an eight-year-boy came to be spared under the searchlights in Płaszów.

When our canvas-covered truck drove away from the convent that Christmas morning, Niania ran wildly to Nazi headquarters. Somehow she managed to find out that after Montelupi prison our transport would be taken to the work camp in Płaszów. She ran to tell Jadwiga, the servant woman from Uncle Samuel's household. Jadwiga alerted her Polish fiancé, who worked for the Nazis at the camp. Uncle Samuel had been put to use designing bridges and viaducts for the Nazis. The commandant of the camp depended on the Jewish architect-engineer. When we were brought to Płaszów, we were on the list of people intended to be shot. Uncle pleaded with the commandant to spare his sister's children. The Nazi relented and made him a gift. We were allowed to stay alive.

Uncle Samuel's privileged status explained why special quarters had been available to Raisa and her mother. It also explained the good food that Jadwiga was able to provide via her fiancé.

Half a century later, in my taste buds there still lurks a memory of the astonishing first chew of smuggled food in that little room. To this day I love to grab a slice of bacon right out of a Saran-wrapped package bought at an American supermarket. I savor the chewy, smoky, velvety taste of silky fat. Or I throw it on a slice of fresh rye bread and smear it with mustard. There are times in my life, when my survival is not threatened, when I reach for the memory of those bites of bacon and for a fleeting instant hold the taste of them on my tongue.

I also recall the shame of being watched by a young man while standing naked, being sponged by Raisa, in a tin tub of warm water that reached only to above my knees. Could that handsome Polish man have been Jadwiga's fiancé?

At the time of my brother's Polish trip Jadwiga was a feisty seventy-year-old widow. With my brother and his wife she traveled to Israel to be honored by Yad Vashem. She made a fine speech in Polish. In it she told how as a young woman she had run away from a cruel, primitive life in her peasant home.

"In *pan* Samuel and *pani* Bella's house," she said, "was the first time in my life that I was not treated like an animal. I loved that family. I wish I could have done more. I wish I could have saved them."

If, on that January evening in 1945 on the march out of Płaszów, I had trusted my cousin, her father would not have been kicked to death at the camp of Bergen Belsen. Her mother would not have died of a raging fever. Jadwiga had come for them at a designated spot. And Niania had come for us. Because of a ten-year-old's fear and distrust, I could not be convinced to step out without my brother. By her mother's side my cousin stayed on the march. Resigned. Hoping.

How could I have known that in January the Nazis had been defeated everywhere except in Poland and in parts of Eastern Europe? That they were fleeing, taking their prisoners with them to escape the Russian Army that was rapidly coming closer, marching across Poland toward Germany, where the Americans were closing in from the west? Did any of the grown-ups know that? Years after the war was over, I learned that Kraków was liberated only days after our march out of Płaszów. Why did these tired Nazis bother to drag us along with them and hang on to us until the camps were liberated in May? All I knew that evening was that it was dark, that we were in the woods, that my brother was not by my side, and that we were surrounded by guards always ready to shoot.

Raisa did survive. She went to Israel. She married another survivor who was a house painter. They had a son and a daughter. In a photograph, with her grown, handsome Sabra children by her side, a stocky, sturdy woman with close-cropped hair, a Jewish woman in a Jewish land, looks soberly into the camera.

More than fifty years have passed since I survived the times and places of the dreaded words *deportation, concentration camp, liquidation.* Newspapers and television programs are full of recollections of those years. There are documentaries and debates and memorials and countless heartbreaking accounts of what happened during the years of terror and hunger and humiliation. So many people who managed to live through those times are now dead. My mother and father are dead. They lie buried side by side in a modest, peaceful plot of earth in a cemetery in New Jersey.

Settled into my life in America, I have tried to learn from those around me and close to me how to live it. With family and friends I have lived through joyful times and regrets and sadness and betrayals, times that have knocked me down and also given me strength. Work has brought me great, multifaceted satisfaction. Music and theater and books and playing with words in the English language toss me into a forever changing kaleidoscope of surprises.

As an American traveling in Europe I am a tourist looking at famous places that I never had a chance to visit before I became an American. When, after only a few sleepy hours on a jet plane from New York, I land in London or Paris or Rome, I think of the furtive ride in a hay wagon, the escape from Niania's village on the old train, and the few steps of a frightening walk across a bridge that then loomed as a dangerous enormous distance. Going through passport control at airports, I present my American passport to some weary uniformed official, who sits in a clean Plexiglas booth, hardly gives me a look when he says good morning or *bonjour* or *buon giorno,* and does not point a gun at me. And I sadly think of a time when crossing a checkpoint with a forged piece of paper could mean escape or capture, life or death. When in Europe I am asked where I am from, I love to be able to say, "I am an American." And no matter what great touristy fun I have had, I am happy to say good-bye and go home.

I have never gone back to Poland. I have no wish to stand on the grounds of the preserved remains of Auschwitz or Płaszów or Ravensbrück, as if I were paying a visit to tourist attractions not unlike London Bridge or the Roman Forum or the Eiffel Tower.

I have gone back to my beloved Sweden. I still speak Swedish. But the language I used to speak so excellently when I took my first civilizing steps as a young girl has to be wakened from its veiled sleep.

In my grown-up life when available choices tug at me and challenge, I think of the quiet, decent simplicity of those months I spent in the Swedish sanatorium. I had never before experienced such peace. Poland. War. The Nazis. Niania. I didn't really understand what an eccentric, fanatic presence she had been until I was older, until I had children of my own. Even before the Germans came, I had come to accept Niania's religious fervor, her headaches, her weeping, the confusions of her exaggerated love for my brother and me. "What nice little feet!" she would murmur. "What sweet, curved eyebrows!" There were times she decided that someone looking at me had given me the evil eye. She would quickly lick my eyes with her tongue, leaving a sticky film of saliva on my face. Niania never really let us forget that we were not baptized, that we were Jewish children. She worshiped the Holy Mother, mistrusted Jews, yet she protected my brother and me with the flapping wings of a demented angel.

I am a grandmother now. That October afternoon in 1939 in Kraków, when I still had a grandmother, when I knew nothing of journeys in boxcars, I was five years old. I was ten years old when I climbed onto a boxcar transport. I think of my grandmother on one of those trains. Almost certainly separated from Grandfather, she had to have been crammed, sorted, pushed into a barracks with hundreds of other women, shouted at, forced to take off her clothes. Somewhere the old woman who had made her daughters learn proper German had been stripped naked and shoved and humiliated by strapping young German soldiers. Or perhaps she had just been made to keep the lines moving in an orderly manner. Or was she dragged along the ground like the woman in our transport to Płaszów? I can picture it. I will never know.

In the end what is there to say? I was born far, far away, on a bloody continent at a terrible time. I lived there for a while. I live here now. My love for this country grows with my years. My life has been good. I want more.

Mine is only another story.

ACKNOWLEDGMENTS

To begin with I am grateful to the writers in Jill Hoffman's group whose astute comments served as an early, encouraging impetus in the writing of this book. Thank you, Jill. Also Jennifer Belle, Doug Dorph, Shannon Hammann, Alice Jurish, John Penn, Shelley Steenhouse, Robert Steward, Emily West, and Harry Waitzman.

I want to thank many librarians and teachers, who after hearing capsule versions of the beginnings of my life said countless times, "You really ought to write about this."

A warm thanks to all my friends at the Richland County Public Library in Columbia, South Carolina, especially to Ginger Shuler, Leslie Barban, Judy McClendon, and David Warren, who were among the first to hear me read an excerpt at an event at their library.

A special thanks to my friends Emily McCully, Elizabeth Diggs, William Grey, and Virginia and Tom Smith, to whom I read bits and pieces and who urged me on. To my friends Ruth and John Rublowsky and Nancy and John Berry, who all nagged me to do it. To my friends Barbara Flood, Joseph Myers, and Bill Tivenan, who listened to my complaints and moaning in good grace. Also to Alison Courtney Holt and John Threadgill.

To my dear friend Allan Manning, who said wise things about books and writing when I, full of doubts, faltered.

To William Giles, ever funny, encouraging, and trusting, cool and patient with suggestions and help in producing presentable and organized manuscript pages.

A warm thanks to Dr. Verne Moberg and Professor Anna Frajlich-Zajac, both of Columbia University in New York City, for their expert advice on German, Swedish, and Polish usage and translations.

As always I would like to thank all my associates and friends at Greenwillow Books: Lori Benton, Jazan Higgins, Virginia Duncan, Tara Filaski, Phyllis Larkin, Sylvie Le Floc'h, Robin Roy, Amira Rubin, Elizabeth Shub, Barbara Trueson, and Ava Weiss.

And lastly, an astonished thank-you to my great friend, editor, and publisher Susan Hirschman, who said yes.

NO PRETTY PICTURES

A CHILD OF WAR

Coming to New York

Coming to New York

In the rough seas of late December, on the old Swedish liner *Gripsholm*, we were crossing the Atlantic to America. The first two days I had been seasick. And angry at my parents, angry at my younger brother. Angry at myself, too, for having gone along with this determined emigration. I was almost seventeen. I could have found a way to stay behind. Swedish people had taken care of me before. I would not have been kicked out.

Mother and father and brother were not seasick. They were full of plans for our future life in America. In New York City, there were cousins whose parents had gone to America from Poland even before the First World War. Family. Family that was alive. We would be welcomed by these relations, who had managed to be spared from the Nazi monsters. They would be so happy to have new survived relatives in their midst. From them, love and money would come our way. My parents were pinning so much hope on these distant cousins. Father expected to open a candy store or a luncheonette. That had not been possible in the very regulated world of Stockholm, Sweden. My brother would go to university. I would meet a Jewish boy to marry. Maybe a doctor.

These fantasies were not for me. I had no interest in these second or third cousins. All the good things in my life had come from people who were not blood relations. I had left beautiful Stockholm. I had left my friends. I had left my love Sven behind.

Sven and I were Communists. He was a worker in a steel mill. That was real. And honorable. I was an artist. In my paintings I would celebrate strong, muscular men and women at work.

In a corner of the old ship's still somewhat elegant wood-paneled salon, at a writing desk, I dipped my pen in an ink bottle and poured flowery thoughts onto page after page of the ship's "Svenska America Linjen" stationery: "My love, my dearest one. I will remain true to you. I will love you forever. I will come back to you. I will, I must. Or, you must come and take me away. Together we sail to our Sverige. We will be married and live high on a mountaintop with the music of Swedish winds murmuring in the pines, my love, my only one." On and on and on.

My brother was sick of my moping. "Aren't you even a little curious about America?" Two years younger than I, he was playing smart and grown-up. I resented him for being such a good boy. Always taking sides against me with Mother and Father.

"Svenskarna have been good to us for seven years," I snapped at him. "You are gloating about leaving a lovely country and its good people behind."

When I got used to the heaving and rolling of the ship and was no longer seasick, I stood on the deck in my new gray coat and the scarf I had knit, watching the prow cleave

2

the waves. Watching the blue and black water burst into white spray. I was used to being surrounded by waterways. I had been on school trips aboard small boats and ferries in between islands in the archipelago surrounding Stockholm. Since the ferry crossing on the Baltic when my brother and I had been liberated from concentration camp, I had never been out of sight of land. The idea of *faraway* or *somewhere* would end when we reached the horizon at the end of this voyage. Once again, I would have to try to speak a new language and find new ways to be.

I had read stories about outward-bound Swedes, escaping poverty and hunger and settling into other hardships in America. I had read Joseph Conrad. In the Hollywood musicals I had seen with my girlfriends, sea voyages were drenched in moonlight. Movie stars in evening clothes danced to sleek dance bands. Hollywood musicals were about glitter and glamour and romance. Stormy winter seas were not in season in those movies.

I knew other things about America. My friends and I had listened to phonograph records of Stan Kenton and Nat King Cole. With my friends, I had hung out in a dance hall where local bands played Dixieland. We hugged the walls, worried that no boy would come forward to ask for a dance.

I had gone to the Royal Dramatic Theater and seen English and French classic plays in translation. I had seen the new American play everyone was talking about—*En handels resandes dod* (*Death of a Salesman*). I knew that people made fun of a place called Brooklyn.

3

EXTRAS

I knew words to many American popular songs: "Mona Lisa," "My Foolish Heart," "What'll I Do (When You Are Far Away)." As a good-bye present, Sven had given me an American songbook. "Oh I wish I were in de land ob cotton, long time dere am not forgotten . . ." The ending of the verses, "Look away, Dixieland," was very odd, and "de" and "ob" and "dere" really confused me. What the "Dixieland" in this book had to do with the band music my friends and I had listened and danced to, I had no clue.

Some days into the voyage, I had gone into the rather gloomily lit lounge, heading for the writing desk in order to write yet another letter to Sven, when I was surprised to run into a Polish girl whom I had known five years before at the youth camp outside of Stockholm. She spoke first.

"Don't you remember?" She spoke in Polish. "From Polish camp in Kummelnas." Oh, yes. Though she looked tired and sallow and shapeless in a brown wool dress, sunk into the armchair with fraying velvet upholstery, I did recognize her. I remembered her limp blondish hair. And how she had tried to disguise its thinnesss by putting it up in paper curlers every single night. Her hair looked straight and short and not curled. She held a baby in her lap. Another small child was hanging onto her knees.

"Marysia! Of course I remember," I cried. Marysia, along with several other girls, had been my roommate.

After I had been discharged from the tuberculosis sanatorium, I had lived in that holding tank for displaced Polish kids for three months. I was twelve then. She was a few

4

years older. Probably fifteen. I suppose we had been friends. I had no real idea of what it was to be a friend. The war had taken care of that.

I remember one time we had been given some pocket money by the camp counselors. Marysia and I and another girl got permission to take the bus to Stockholm. We went to the movies—the dark and mysterious *Humoresque*, with Joan Crawford and John Garfield. The girls spoke no Swedish. I had to translate the Swedish subtitles.

When we came out of the movie theater on one of Stockholm's central streets, some Swedish teenage boys started following us. *"Hejsan, tjejer. Skall vi följa med?"*

Marysia and the other girl started to laugh and flirt with the boys. But they didn't understand what the boys were saying. I did. I understood the Swedish slang. They kept repeating one word over and over.

"What are they saying? Tell us." Marysia and her friend wanted me to translate. "What do they want?" The boys were not interested in me. Too shy and too embarrassed, not even sure I knew the word in Polish, I just wanted to get away from them.

"I don't understand them," I lied. "They are speaking Danish."

When my parents finally got their visas and left Poland to come to Sweden, I was not sorry to leave the youth camp and all of its inhabitants behind. Eventually the reasons for the camp passed, and the place was closed.

The kids had either found relatives and gone back to

5

EXTRAS

Poland or found Swedish foster homes. The older ones had probably just gone to work. That is what Marysia had done, she told me. She also started going steady with one of the boys from the camp. She was sixteen at the time. He eighteen. In a town not far from Stockholm, Marysia had worked in a dairy plant. Janek had worked on an assembly line in a bicycle plant. They got married.

During those five years I had been going to school. I had had piano lessons and gone to evening classes at an art school.

I remembered Janek. He had been one of the boys who had consistently taunted and bullied the one other Jewish girl at the camp. And he had been one of the gang that had doused me with a bucketful of cold water on Easter morning.

Now that I was sufficiently distant from Poland and the war years, I didn't mind admitting to myself how constantly frightened I had really been of all those Polish kids. And how I had distanced myself from the Jewish girl. I was a Catholic. I participated in the Mass and knew all the church songs and prayers. Still, there was that time when the new Polish scout uniforms had arrived at the camp. I was sure that I would be denied the uniform and cap because I was not really Polish. I had been convinced that I would not be given a uniform and cap to join the others in scout maneuvers because I was Jewish.

At almost seventeen, I was an informed egalitarian. My hair was long. I wore it in a ponytail. I was wearing a black skirt and black stockings and new black flat shoes. I knew that that was how the Existentialist girls in Paris dressed. I had been told by savvy Swedish friends that I looked like Juliette Gréco. Or the actress Maria Casarès, whom my friends and I had just seen in the French movie *Orphée*.

"Remember that night when we came out of the movies on Kungsgatan?" I tried to reach for a shared memory of girlish fun. "I lied to you," I said. "I knew what those Swedish guys were saying."

I looked at the older Marysia and the two children. "I'm still too embarrassed to translate what they suggested."

She remembered and laughed. The baby boy on her lap started to cry. Marysia stuck a bottle in his mouth. The kid started to suck rhythmically.

"Your babies are sweet," I said.

Marysia gave me a weary smile.

"And now we are both going to America," I said, trying to sound breezy and carefree. "To New York City."

"No, I am going to Canada," Marysia said. "To Montreal." She pronounced it "Maantreal."

"Janek's uncle had a butcher shop," she went on. "He vouched for us. Janek is working for him already."

After that encounter, I didn't run into Marysia again. She was never around in the evening to play chess or cards. She didn't come to the New Year's Eve celebration or the captain's dinner. Just before continuing to New York, our ship docked late one night in Nova Scotia. Snow was failing. From an upper deck I watched Marysia struggling

EXTRAS

down the gangplank with her bundles and her babies.

Toward the end of the crossing—and maybe because of my encounter with Marysia—I began to think that if I had to be emigrating to America, it was nicer to be with a mother and a father and a brother and a portfolio of drawings than sailing to Canada with mewling babies to meet a husband who was a butcher in training.

And I began to prize the temporary suspension between two worlds. To have meals served regularly by stewards at a big round table. A bathroom with a shower in our cabin. Compared with the meager comforts of the little house we had lived in just outside of Stockholm, where my brother and father had to light a wooden fire to get a heater going in the cellar to get hot water, where we washed in a basin in the kitchen, this was luxury.

Mother and Father met another emigrating Jewish couple and their son, who had relatives in New Jersey. Their eighteen-year-old, Simon, had a scholarship to Howard University. He was interested in American history. I had never thought of history as being anything but European or Swedish. The Thirty Years' War. Queen Kristina. I loved reading about the eighteenth-century Swedish king Gustav III, and I had visited his palace at Drottningholm.

I took time off from composing letters to Sven. I sat in the salon with my charcoal and drawing paper and sketched my brother and Simon playing chess. Two male heads lowered over a chessboard, arms bent at the elbows, hands supporting chins. My parents played cards with their new friends.

8

Sometimes after dinner a small combo played dance music. I had one fancy dress I had made of dark green taffeta. I danced with Simon or my brother. Even with my father.

Even though I wasn't going to admit it, I began to have a good time. I had begun to think that perhaps this was not all wrong. Perhaps in the world that people lived in now, almost seven years after the war, I could come to a new place and know it and then go back to the place I had left. I had to go away to know what going back was like. That was what I was doing, wasn't it? I might have to stay a while, of course. Since America was full of money, I would get some, somehow. As soon as I did, I would return to Sweden—when I wanted to, when I decided to. When I was ready, I would sail back to my lover and my friends.

On a cold and dazzling January morning, the fourteen-day voyage was coming to an end. Amidst the waking toots and blasts of the harbor, we all gathered on the deck of the creaky old ocean liner to greet a sunlit Statue of Liberty. Manhattan Island was coming closer. The reality of the tall buildings that I knew only as flat black-and-white images on movie screens and postcards thrilled me.

What a glorious sight! I could not help admitting it. Everyone on deck was smiling, laughing. People were embracing each other. My mother had tears in her eyes. "We will have family again," she sighed.

Maybe it was all possible. All right, maybe. After all, this was the first time in my life that I was arriving at a place with a family group who had paid for tickets to travel.

We were not fleeing danger. We were not being displaced on command. We were not unwanted refugees. We were legitimate travelers who had decided to come to a new place to live. Maybe the chilly winds blending industrial smells of smoke and harbor oil spills were blowing promises in our direction.

Sweden's ocean liners had their own berth in New York. Svenska Amerika Linjen. Swedish American Line, pier 57. When the tugboats had finally guided us in and the old ship dropped its anchor, I was overwhelmed by the reality of how far away I was from the place I had taken for granted as my home. On the main deck simple fold-out tables had been set up. This was the checkpoint for passports and visas and all the documents my parents carried and now began to fumble with. I had not given a thought to them in the daily life on shipboard. All four of us had small suitcases with clothes and personal things we had kept in the cabin. I held on to my art portfolio. The rest of our luggage was being carted up by stevedores from the bowels of the ship.

We waited to be beckoned forward by uniformed officials. Waited. Shuffling, nervous, to present our passports. To reclaim our boxes and suitcases and ourselves and enter that world that was anything but flat celluloid. The city that waited in three dimensions, in color, with buildings that really looked as if they scraped the sky. No such architecture had risen where we came from. From where we stood on the deck, the jagged, tightly stacked massive city seemed less penetrable, less airy and glowing than it had looked at a distance when we had slowly sailed into the harbor. But inside that density there had to be streets like those in any other city. And space and people, breathing, living, making noise, making things. And louder than the city I had left—I could feel the smaller, more measured sounds and shapes of my life increase in volume. All I wanted was permission to walk away from the controls and the fussing with our papers. To go over there, at last, away from the moored old ship and have my feet step on the pavement of the famous city.

"There they are!" Mother cried. She waved and pointed in the direction of five people standing in a little clump. "The cousins are here." Three women and two men, all of them wearing hats and glasses, all of them unsmiling behind a roped-off area on the dock. I knew that the two maiden ladies and their brother had been born in New York. I did not think that they could speak Polish. In my head, I was trying to stack up some English phrases. "How do you do?" Such an oddity. How do they do what? Why ask somebody, before you know them, "how" they "do"? I had to have something, some opening phrase ready. I picked out words I had learned and lined them up, as if for inspection. I wanted something in English to roll off my tongue. "Our ocean journey was rather good."

Then I remembered that the married couple cousins were originally from Poland, via Germany—came here just before the Anschluss. They must still speak Polish, I thought. From

11

behind tables of officials and policemen, I did not sense much of a joyful welcome.

I glanced again at our piles of luggage collected in a corner. Two old, old leather suitcases, bulging. Some boxes. One had silver my parents had bought. Another one contained my little Singer sewing machine. I saw my box of Swedish books wrapped with twine and brown paper that was tearing. I clutched my passport—and my portfolio, as if it were another passport.

Ahead of us, I saw Simon and his parents present their passports and documents. They were quickly waved on. I saw a porter follow them with their boxes and suitcases already loaded on a handcart. He followed them down the gangplank. A man and a woman rushed toward the threesome, smiling. Kisses, hugs. I could hear their laughter. Soon the happy group and their possessions were piled into a rather substantial vehicle with nice wooden paneling on the sides.

They looked back in our direction. They waved and smiled. I heard the hum of the motor. By the time the car started to drive away from the dock, their heads were no longer turned toward us. The four of us stood there. Trapped, suspended, left behind.

From behind the temporary official desk, questions were coming fast. "Co mowia. Co to znaczy?" What is he saying? What does this mean? Already my parents were gearing up, depending on me and my brother for translations. Catching only half a phrase here and there, I could hardly keep up.

My parents' English was virtually nonexistent. My properly British-accented school English was defeated by the New York speech of the official who was gruffly investigating our papers. Nobody cared about the quality of my ocean journey. From the group of cousins, the one with the especially thick Coke-bottle glasses volunteered to come forward. The husband of the couple, who had left Germany in the nick of time, followed. He had thick lips and froggish eyes. He embraced my mother. He looks like Edward G. Robinson, I thought, reassuring myself with a moment of smartness from my storage bin of American references. The cousin spoke English well enough, from what I could tell. But in trying to appear authoritative, he began to bristle at the immigration official, which did not help. It was then that the somewhat more calm and pinched, more well-spoken American lady cousin in the thick glasses intervened. Between the two they finally understood what was not right.

The health certificates that we needed to be cleared for entrance to the United States were insufficient. The Edward G. Robinson cousin explained the problem in Polish. My brother and I had been sick with tuberculosis after the war. My parents had not bothered to clear with health authorities in Stockholm that we had been hale and hearty for several years.

All the old shame that usually stayed tucked in was bursting all over me. How could my parents have been so stupid and not taken care of these things? And then putting their trust in this homely, ineffectual group of elderly relatives, who could do nothing to help us cross the barriers that kept us rooted in refugee, refuse status! How could I have been so stupid, so passive, to have followed my parents like a sheep? That's what people did during the war. Obeyed and followed and lay down to be slaughtered.

All at once I was overwhelmed with the reality of this cold morning, the giant noisy city we were about to step into. Earlier, standing on the deck with all the other passengers when the Statue of Liberty majestically came into view, I had been swept up in the excitement of my parents, my brother, and all those other passengers who had gathered on deck, not wanting to miss this moment. All that was gone now. Shame and anger were back. When I had gone with my mother to the Polish consulate in Stockholm to get a visa stamped into my passport, I had thought that I was following some legal routine for non-Swedes—but I had never wanted to believe that this journey would actually take place. Now I was trapped on the deck of a Swedish ship docked at pier 57 in the harbor of New York City, surrounded by Americans who resolutely kept us behind their barriers. The last few days on the ship I had seduced myself by staging in my head a vision of a festive welcome, something that if not exactly accompanied by trumpet blasts from *Aida*, at least would be theatrical and celebratory. I was a smart girl with a portfolio, I had studied art and languages and literature. I was prepared to drop a few well-phrased remarks in English. And soon after that, I would start making arrangements for a return journey. I thought of all the letters I had been writing

14

to my love and my friends. I had given them to the steward in charge of telegraph and communications. "They will sail with us safely back to Sverige," he had assured me. How I wished he could take me back too!

In Stockholm, for five years I had become used to a kind of belonging. And here I was, right back to being an outcast. Why had I agreed to come? Why, why? Why had I even been fooled into having a good time during the crossing? It was as if I had willed a guarantee of a rational and good temporary transition in my life. I was furious and cold and felt more helpless and betrayed and ineffectual than I had for years. I couldn't go back to Sweden. I had no money to buy a ticket. And who knew if my papers were even valid to let me back in?

One thing was clear. Our luggage would be kept, and we would be detained. We were not to be allowed to enter New York City, whose screech and noise was a malicious tease in the background. A small dark van with NEW YORK CITY PORT AUTHORITY written on the side waited for us on the dock, with two policemen. I walked down the gangplank behind my mother. Her gloved hand holding onto the protective side rope irritated me. My father's hat and briefcase irritated me even more. The relatives hovered together on the dock. My mother made a resigned grimace. My father took off his hat and nodded slightly in their direction. I said nothing when we all climbed into the vehicle.

We were driven along the waterway that had carried our boat to pier 57; huge liners and merchant ships were docked.

Cranes hovered. Dock workers lifted crates, wheeled cargo, and shouted. Barges and tugboats exploded their noises from the water, blending them with the rest of the dense rumble and screech of taxis and trucks and buses on land.

"I hear America singing." I had read portions of Whitman's poem in my English class. I had never imagined that the port of New York would be so immense. This was not Stockholm, with its Skepsholmen and Blasieholmen and quays, with their fishing boats and ferries gently tied up and the occasional roundness of a melodious toot. Until an hour ago, I had thought that I had lived in a very large city. I had thought that I knew things. That I spoke English. That the years in Stockholm had scrubbed down the rot of the war and revived the frightened and confused little girl with a bit of spit and polish and given her some sheen around the edges. Now, because of a few words missing from an official paper, we were being taken to a prison. I had heard of it. The tired and poor and powerless were taken there—to the place called Ellis Island.